Apples

Apples

❖

WRITTEN & ILLUSTRATED BY

ROGER YEPSEN

W. W. NORTON & COMPANY

NEW YORK   LONDON

Apples
was designed by Katy Homans
typeset by Michael & Winifred Bixler
and
printed and bound by South China Printing Company

Library of Congress Cataloging-in-Publication Data

Yepsen, Roger B.
Apples / by Roger Yepsen.
p.   cm.
Includes bibliographical references.
1. Apples—Varieties.   2. Apples—Pictorial works.   3. Apples.
4. Cookery (Apples)   I. Title.
SB363.3.A1Y46   1994
641.3'411—dc20   94–15688

ISBN 0–393–03690–1
W. W. Norton & Company, Inc., 500 Fifth Avenue, New York, N.Y. 10110
W. W. Norton & Company Ltd., 10 Coptic Street, London WC1A 1PU

1 2 3 4 5 6 7 8 9 0

To my uncle Rhodes Copithorn,
who was inspired by the great old Northern Spies
in his Long Island backyard
to look for an orchard of his own;

to my grandfather Defoe Mosher,
who grew Jonathans, Winesaps, Northern Spies, Rhode Island
Greenings, and Grimes Golden on his Indiana farm;

and to my great-grandmother Edna Bloom Carter,
who made pies from the two unpruned Yellow Transparents
behind her house.

CONTENTS

❖   ❖   ❖

Akane · Arkansas Black · Arlet · Ashmead's Kernel
Baldwin · Belle de Boskoop · Ben Davis
Black Gilliflower · Blue Permain · Braeburn
Bramley's Seedling · Calville Blanc
Chenango Strawberry · Cornish Gilliflower
Cortland · Cox's Orange Pippin · Criterion · Elstar
Empire · Esopus Spitzenburg · Fallawater
Fameuse · Fireside · Freyberg
Fuji · Gala · Golden Delicious
Golden Russet · GoldRush · Granny Smith
Gravenstein · Grimes Golden · Haralson
Hawaii · Holstein · Honeygold

Hubbardston Nonesuch · Hudson's Golden Gem
Hyslop Crab · Idared · Jonagold · Jonalicious
Jonamac · Jonathan · Kandil Sinap
Keepsake · Kidd's Orange Red · King David
King Luscious · Knobbed Russet
Lady · Liberty · McIntosh · Macoun · Maiden Blush
Melrose · Mollie's Delicious · Mutsu
Newtown Pippin · New York 429 · Northern Spy
Northwestern Greening · Ozark Gold
Paradise · Pink Pearl · Pitmaston Pineapple
Prairie Spy · Red Delicious
Rhode Island Greening · Rome Beauty
Roxbury Russet · Senshu · Spartan · Spigold
Stayman · Summer Rambo · SunCrisp
Swaar · Tompkins King
Twenty Ounce · Tydeman's Early · Wagener
Wealthy · Westfield Seek-No-Further
White Winter Pearmain · Winesap
Winter Banana · Wolf River · Yellow Bellflower
York Imperial · Zabergau Reinette

I. THE FRUIT OF LEGEND
AND LUNCHBOXES

❖   ❖   ❖

Apples. Red, round, crisp, and cool.

The list of adjectives doesn't have to stop there. An apple can be much more than the generic red orb we've come to expect from the supermarket's produce department.

The orchards of North America have produced well over a thousand named apple varieties. Each one, with its characteristic color, heft, and aura, is as distinctive as a gemstone. Some apples are mysterious and hard to get to know. Others are as accessible as a carrot.

There are fruity apples tasting of banana, mango, pineapple, and pear, and spicy apples tasting of licorice, cinnamon, coriander, rue, and nutmeg. Apples can be had candy sweet or cider sour, cleanly astringent or mild-mannered, and hard as a raw potato or messy as a peach.

The best-known varieties tend to be quite round and smooth. But others are shaped like toy tops or lopsided old pillows and may have skins that look scarred and unpalatable to the unaccustomed eye. A few, such as the homely Knobbed Russet, don't look like apples at all. Sizes vary from the crabs, each just an inch across, to branch-bending giants the size of a baby's head and weighing well over a pound.

Colors range from near white to forgettable beige to the deep, waxy near black of a showroom limo. And that's not to mention the reds, in uncountable shades, patterns, and levels of opacity and luminosity. An apple's red coat overlies a layer of yellow or ocher or green that will either set the apple ablaze or mute it. A Stayman's red is transposed to a minor key by the green pigment below. But on a Winter Banana or Ozark Gold, the red blush acts like a lens, incandescing with the light that reflects up through it.

Many apples are pedigreed, as their names suggest. Esopus Spitzenburg, Cox's Orange Pippin, and Duchess of Oldenburg are pomological royalty. The newer varieties have yet to acquire folklore status and tend to sound like supermarket products (Splendor, Sundowner), corporate mergers (Delcon) or, worse still, hybrid tomatoes (Pink Satin, Red Baron, Nova Easygro).

Apples have the diversity, lore, and subtlety of good wine. But in North America that great wealth has been wasted on most of us, most of the time. As apple customers we pick vanilla when presented with a choice of apples. Even 250 apples.

That's a rough count of the varieties offered by Fred Janson's roadside apple business outside Rockton, Ontario. In a lifetime Americans sample an average of six. So, how do customers respond to this man's cornucopia?

"Of the people who stop here," Janson says, "maybe ninety-five percent want McIntosh or Yellow Delicious or one of the supermarket apples."

The long winter of our indifference has extinguished hundreds of quirky and appealing apple varieties, and made others almost impossible to find. The names remain to suggest what once was there for the picking: Bascombe's Mystery, Stump of the World, Horneburger Pancake (one slice filled a pan). We've made do with supermarket apples that have been chosen less for flavor than for bright, cheery color and sturdiness in transit. That's why Red Delicious, Golden Delicious, and McIntosh, making up more than half of the apples grown in the United States, routinely lose taste tests to apples you've never heard of.

OUR FRUITED PLAIN

It has not always been this way. America once was a land of apple lovers. The favorite varieties of our colonial heroes have become well-known details of their biographies. George Washington's most famous horticultural exploit may have been leveling a cherry tree, but as an adult he built a distillery for making apple brandy and was a fan of Newtown Pippins. Benjamin Franklin liked this apple so much that he had barrels of them shipped to England while lobbying there for the colonies. John Adams is said to have begun each day with a tankard of cider and was moved to write an ode to the beverage. Thomas Jefferson identified Esopus Spitzenburg as his pick of the apple varieties grown in the hilly orchards of Monticello.

Free-sowing Johnny Appleseed became a fixture of American folklore. His apples might not have been impressive—the seeds of a great variety rarely grow up into anything special—but his spirit outlived his trees. Meanwhile, out in the orchards thousands of unsung amateurs were experimenting with promising varieties. Any fencerow seedling was a potential candidate for a new name and local renown. In fact, most of our varieties are love children, the products of chance pollination between unknown parents a century ago. Every region had several of these apples, each with its special talents: flavor, aroma, picking time, storability, resistance to disease. There were famous cider apples, baking apples, sauce apples, drying apples, and dessert apples.

Before mechanical refrigeration was used to prolong the life of produce, families bought a succession of seasonal favorites from summer through late fall, when the long-keeping winter apples could carry them through midsummer. One British visitor to the new United States remarked that apples were available eleven months of the year. And apples were consumed year-round as cider, America's most popular drink among rich and poor, young and old.

Apples could be both a staple food and an object of connoisseurship. At rural kitchen tables, apple pies and tarts were served as routinely as bread. And the better city restaurants served dessert apples in little individual boxes, stem and two leaves attached, with a card noting variety and grower.

Before the time when Americans became identified as fans of sports teams, they were known for their favorite apples. People were even described as apples: crabs, bad apples, apple polishers, apples of one's eye. To describe the narrow, ingrown persona of small-town Americans, novelist Sherwood Anderson came up with "twisted apples."

By 1900 a thousand varieties were sold in America's markets. But changes were under way that were to consign most of those apples to obscurity.

THE REDDENING OF AMERICA

The squandering of our great apple heritage has been laid at the pesticide-spattered work boots of modern orchardists. It has been said they would rather market a few easy-to-ship apples than bother with an orchard full of antique oddballs.

That's a simple explanation, and not a very good one. It ignores the curious thing that happened to us consumers when we glimpsed perfection in the form of a flawless, waxen, carmine apple—the perfection that chemicals have made possible. Having partaken of this gorgeous fruit, we would accept no less. Spotted, modest-size, off-red apples now looked flawed or damaged. And so it was that growers became hooked on a regimen of spraying the daylights out of a few highly marketable varieties. Mechanical refrigeration further reduced the number of apples sold, by allowing a handful of varieties to be stored forever and shipped anywhere.

If commercial orchardists were to be faulted for anything, it was for following good business practice. The push for maximum yields per acre and efficient production slighted apples that weren't round enough, big enough, or tough enough. In the new order, a key advantage of a variety was that it have a long stem, to permit better penetration by sprays. Another was that it be "typy," industry lingo for an apple that closely mimics a nationally known variety and can ride on its coattails.

The apples that didn't fit were abandoned. In New England, home to more pomological treasures than any other region of the continent, agriculture agents and growers agreed to focus on marketing just seven varieties—seven, out of the hundreds that had been developed and tended for centuries. Countless old, idiosyncratic orchards were ripped out.

The symbol of the way we've come to grow and enjoy apples is Red Delicious, America's top banana. It was a marketer's dream. Red Delicious won few taste contests, but it kept up its cheerful, lipstick red exterior even after the insides had turned to a mush that tasted like old snow. Inspired by Big Red's success, government fruit experts strove to turn other, less glamorous varieties into Delicious look-alikes, developing strains that were ever more red and resilient. In 1959 a government guide to apple production coached growers that "sales may be increased 75 percent on the average by increasing the area of solid red color from 15 to 50 percent."

Americans gradually forgot what a really good, fresh apple tastes like, just as they came to prefer fake maple syrup to real. The industry ideal, says Tom Burford, a grower with five hundred varieties growing around his Virginia farmhouse, was not a spotless fruit but the unvarying sheen of *plastic*.

Not surprisingly the American appetite for apples languished. There were other reasons as well. Refrigeration had allowed the farm orchard to grow into an agribusiness. But the big chill also opened the United States and Canada to fruits that were once rare novelties and luxuries for a few. The apple, king of the temperate zones, was dethroned as America's favorite fruit by the orange.

We now eat an average of just eighteen pounds of fresh apples a year—less than an apple a week. Belgians and Italians put away three times that amount. And *they* fall short of the Dutch, who approach the health maxim's ideal of an apple a day. Europeans have an international reputation as discriminating apple eaters who pay more attention to munching than to marketing. We Americans, in contrast, continue to be known for our unwavering allegiance to red, round, and sweet.

Not long ago one of the state agricultural experiment stations introduced a new variety with a real personality, Jonagold, and apple experts confidently predicted it would succeed—in Europe. They forecast little interest for Jonagold in the United States, where produce managers and shoppers alike seem puzzled by apples that aren't all red, all yellow, or all green.

AN APPLE RENAISSANCE

Fortunately the story doesn't end there. Just as we Americans have let it be known we'll no longer settle for shoddy cars and light beers, so we are defying prediction by hunting for apples we weren't supposed to like—fruits that might not be picture-perfect but that promise gustatory adventure. The same families who embrace dark imported beer and Toyotas have welcomed exceptional varieties from abroad—among them Mutsu and Fuji from Japan and Braeburn from New Zealand. None is as gorgeously red as a Red Delicious. But any of them will knock off that variety in a taste test, every time.

This savvier crop of apple eaters is also looking into just

what sorts of chemicals are used on fruit. They're concerned that a supermarket apple is sprayed an average of twelve times on the tree, that it may be subjected to further treatment in storage, that it likely is embalmed under a protective layer of wax or shellac.

The British have a head start on our apple revival. In Britain the old varieties have become a symbol of resisting the uniformity imposed by three mighty forces: supermarkets, the European Union, and American-style fast food. The Agriculture Ministry is encouraging stores to stock more domestic apple varieties, and some now offer as many as forty. This initiative comes none too early. Roughly two-thirds of Britain's orchards have been lost, and three out of five apples are imported.

In North America government pomologists haven't been deaf to the fuss. They are testing varieties with more concern for taste and developing impressive new disease-resistant varieties that will change the way apples are grown. But the folk heroes of the apple's rebirth are the orchardists rescuing old favorites from extinction, while celebrating the best of the new imports. They wander back roads with pocketknives, borrowing wood from the stocky trees of abandoned orchards to perpetuate a bit of heritage. And they test the American climate and the American sensibility with promising foreign apples.

Perhaps this book will inspire you to explore, too—if not in abandoned orchards, then in the tamer frontier of farmer's markets, greengrocers, roadside stands, and fruit tastings offered at fall festivals across the United States and Canada.

The heart of *Apples* is a gallery of about ninety varieties. You'll find a mix of recent introductions from abroad, newly baptized apples from domestic apple breeders, and highly esteemed antiques treasured by our ancestors and kept available by enthusiasts. Some are well known. Others are obscure and may take a bit of sleuthing before you can get your teeth into a sample. The source listing guides you to a mail-order business that can ship several dozen varieties, including many illustrated in the pages that follow. For those who want to grow their own trees in a pot, against a wall, or out in the yard, there is a list of nurseries that sell the stock of several hundred apples by mail.

Please note that these color portraits are intended to be inspirational—to intrigue you, to coax you into seeking out a few varieties. Because apples are among the most variable of plants, the specimens portrayed here will not be exact duplicates of those you grow or buy. Each painting is of an individual fruit, rather than of a generic composite you'd find in a true field guide.

Another word of caution concerns the written descriptions of each fruit's appeal to the senses. Apples may change greatly in taste and aroma from one season to the next, even from one county to the next. Like wine, they tease and delight us with nuances of taste and aroma. Is that exotic scent mangolike or closer to freshly cut lime? Coriander or pine? Please don't disqualify your own impressions just because they haven't been confirmed in print.

And you needn't feel cheated if you fail to detect the nuances described here. Sometimes an apple just tastes like an apple, and most of the time that's pleasure enough.

2. HOW TO BUY A GOOD APPLE

❖ ❖ ❖

To Henry David Thoreau, ever the grouchy purist, an apple had no spirit if not eaten under the tree from which it was picked. Nevertheless, most of us will continue to shop for apples, and it helps to know something of the apple business. To bite into a good apple, you have to *buy* a good apple.

STRETCHING THE SEASON

Unlike candy bars or linguine, apples are living, breathing organisms. That means they are always changing. An apple eaten today won't taste or smell or feel quite the same as it would have yesterday or might tomorrow. Even in the chilly fastness of your refrigerator's produce bin, its life cycle continues after harvest.

The apple takes in oxygen from the atmosphere and puts out carbon dioxide, most of this gas traveling through small pale vents, called lenticels, that are visible as scattered dots in the skin. Acids are metabolized for energy. Starches are converted to sugars. Colors turn warmer. A sweet fragrance is exhaled. The apple even produces heat.

Collectively these changes are known as ripening. An apple wants to ripen. With a bright face and complex of flavors and perfumes, it can better beguile warm-blooded animals to eat its flesh and scatter its seed and thereby perpetuate the species. Indeed, ripe apples look, smell, and taste best to humans. But ripeness is only another stage. Flavor and crispness are fleeting. Eventually the fruit lose their appeal to the senses.

Growers have a few strategies for stretching an apple's prime. One is to pick the fruit before it's ripe. This serves growers, but not you. Fruit that ripens off the tree may taste starchy and bland, with an uninviting texture, an insipid color, and defects known in the trade as bitter pit and storage scald.

WHAT'S RIPE

A host of changes, some visible and some not, take place in an apple as it ripens.

Skin color: loses green chlorophyll, warming the under-lying skin toward yellow, while orange and red pigments increase.

Flesh: turns softer.   *Astringency: decreases.*
Starch: decreases.   *Flavor and aroma: increase.*
Acidity: decreases.   *Sweetness: increases.*
Juiciness: increases.

Of course, an apple will not be at its best if picked too late either. So-called senescent apples tend to be unpleasantly soft and mealy and are subject to water core, a condition in which the spaces between cells are flooded with sweetish liquid. Late-picked fruit is especially vulnerable to bruising and decay as well.

Another strategy for keeping apples at their best is to slow the ripening process. That's what your refrigerator accomplishes and what cool basements and springhouses did in the past. Low temperatures manage to put an apple in a lower metabolic gear. The mechanism behind cold storage was fully understood rather late in the history of orcharding. That's because the responsible agent is invisible (and perhaps odorless, too, although scientists still disagree about that): ethylene.

Ethylene is a chemical messenger, or *hormone*, generated by the apple to hasten its own ripening. Most plant and animal hormones, such as adrenaline, are liquids. Ethylene is unusual in that it occurs as a gas. Its role as the agent behind ripening wasn't discovered until the 1800s, and even then only by accident. Utilities had been adding ethylene to gas-lighting systems as a means of brightening the flame, and gas leaks seemed to trigger odd changes in nearby plants.

Ripening can be further slowed by increasing levels of carbon dioxide and reducing oxygen, a strategy called controlled-atmosphere (or CA) storage. An ever-greater amount of the crop is treated to it. Washington State now sticks roughly 60 percent of its apples in CA.

APPLES MAKE FAST COMPANY

The ethylene gas emitted by apples acts as a ripening hormone on other plants as well. If you store a number of apples in the refrigerator, you may notice undesirable changes in their neighbors. Carrots become bitter. Potatoes tend to sprout and shrivel. Asparagus toughens. Brown spots may appear on lettuce. And cucumbers turn yellow.

Not that ethylene is all bad. To speed the ripening of a bag of hard tomatoes, slip in an apple, and seal.

By late December and January supermarkets typically sell out of apples from conventional cold storage (called regular-atmosphere storage, or RA). From then on CA fruits are made available. How can you find out if you're getting CA apples instead of cold-storage dregs? Ask. Produce boxes should be marked "CA" if the fruits were held in controlled-atmosphere storage.

As winter wears on, imported apples supplement the CA stock. Fruits from Chile appear as early as February. Gala, from New Zealand, reaches us beginning in March and April, followed by imported Fuji, Braeburn, and Granny Smith in May and June.

To a food shopper, red means good—ripe and flavorful. Whether it be an apple, a tomato, a cherry, a berry, or a cut of beef, red is a signal to eat.

In shopping for apples, however, color can be misleading information. Many highly flavorful varieties never get very red or even display the slightest blush whatsoever. Among the apple experts out to debunk the redness response is postharvest biologist John Fellman, Ph.D., of the University of Idaho. He suspects that redness may be inversely proportional to flavor and aroma. It could be that apples lavishing their energy on an all-red exterior have less to put into flavor and aroma.

A better clue to good eating is the background color under-lying any flashy pigment. Varieties differ greatly, but a deep green may indicate the apple isn't ready to be eaten fresh, and a yellow that has deepened from light and lemony to eggy could betray a fruit that is past its prime.

Don't be put off by russeting, the golden brown, corky texture that spreads over the skin of certain varieties. It is not a disease, although people brought up on smooth, shiny fruit may think otherwise. In times past, before much of the crop was rushed off to cold vaults, russeting was the valued mark of an apple that kept well. Only recently has it come to be regarded as a "defect," to use the industry's term. That's a shame. As a group russets tend to be spicier and have more character than the average apple. Their flavor often develops for several months in storage, lingering through to the following spring.

IS BIG BETTER?

When you are shopping, your hand just naturally seems drawn to the largest apples. Check that impulse. The bigger the apple, the quicker it matures and the more likely firmness and texture are on the way out. And big costs more. You can save money at the supermarket with baggers, fruits culled for their small size and sold in plastic bags. In Washington the state apple commission has marketed undersize fruits as a healthful alternative to junky snacks, calling them "lunchbox-sized" apples.

The size of a given variety will vary from year to year. A key factor is the temperature in the first month and a half after bloom. Cool and cloudy days yield smaller fruits. Most commercial orchards increase size with chemical sprays that cause trees to drop weak, small fruits from the branches in mid-season. This mimics a natural process, called fruit drop, in which the tree sheds some of its immature apples to reserve its resources for the rest. On a smaller scale, growers may thin the trees by hand.

A BUSHEL AND A PECK

Most of us buy our fruit by the pound at the supermarket. You'll pay considerably less if you shop in quantity from growers, and that will introduce you to the arcana of bushels and pecks.

1 bushel = 4 pecks = 42 pounds (approximately)
1 pound = two big apples, or three medium apples, or four small apples

APPLE POLISHING

Most apples look and feel waxy. In fact, that's just what they are. The skin secretes a protective covering of waxes and other forms of cellular fat. This layer serves to hold water in and keep diseases out. Shoppers may confuse the dusty wax coating on an unbuffed apple with chemical residue, and supermarket apples are routinely machine-rubbed to a high gloss. (Note that some apples, such as Golden Delicious, feel dry to the touch and don't take a shine.)

Not all wax jobs are natural. In the 1950s it occurred to a Yakima, Washington, shipper that apples could be waxed just like cars. His mirror-finish apples brought a dollar a box more than untreated fruit, and the practice caught on. As biologist John Fellman puts it, "Even if the apples taste like doodoo, if they look nice and shiny, they'll sell in certain markets." (Curiously, shoppers in the Northwest have come to prefer fruits that lack a high shine.)

The most commonly used coatings are carnauba wax, from the leaves of a Brazilian palm tree, and shellac, a secretion of an Asian bug. In 1991 the U.S. Food and Drug Administration required fresh-apple marketers to use labels indicating what had been done to the apples, but the law largely has been ignored.

Occasionally you may come upon an apple that feels greasy, even bordering on slimy. That's a natural exudate and is generally a sign of fruits that have been in storage a long while and may taste less than satisfactory. But a few varieties, Arlet and Swaar among them, get slippery to the touch even while in their prime. You can remove much of the coating with water and a paper towel.

The apple, over centuries of cultivation, has been changed radically through the process of selection. Humans honor the biggest, brightest, and sweetest with a place in the orchard and pay less attention to those that come through relatively unscathed by pests and disease.

As a result, most apple varieties would be a ruin by harvest-time unless nursed with an arsenal of chemicals. According to the journal *HortScience*, apples are hit with more chemicals per fruit than any other major food crop, starting before there is anything resembling an apple on the tree. In some regions orchards need nearly a dozen sprayings of fungicide alone. Nine out of ten growers use chemical sprays to thin immature apples and yield bigger fruits at harvest. Other potions include streptomycin and a steroid inhibitor.

While some chemicals stay on the surface, to be rinsed off by rain or postharvest cleaning, so-called systemic substances become part of the apple itself and can't be removed by washing or peeling. Alar, a multipurpose agricultural chemical and suspected carcinogen, is a systemic that inspired a scare in the late 1980s. Another systemic is ethephon, used to thin immature apples for bigger fruit; remarkably, if sprayed on Red Delicious, it causes the apples to lose their famous lobed bottoms.

Agricultural experiment stations are developing varieties with built-in defenses against the common scourges of the orchard. If you are concerned about chemicals on apples, look for Freedom, Liberty, and other resistant varieties. But keep in mind that no apples have as yet been bred with resistance to insects.

WHERE TO SHOP

Roadside stands and farmers' markets are the best places to find a wide variety of fresh, locally grown fruits. An honest grower will guide you to apples that are at their peak—a matter requiring some sophistication if a variety goes from not quite ripe to old age in a couple of weeks.

Picking your own at a commercial orchard, a family tradition in many parts of North America, is endangered by the litigious spirit of our time. One picker's fall could mean death to a business. A Hudson Valley, New York, orchard has come up with a radical way to stay open to the public and avoid lawsuits: A crew goes up the rows each day of the season, lopping off apple-laden limbs with chain saws. You can pick all you want without so much as standing on tiptoe.

Many of us have to make do with the neighborhood supermarket. You can find yourself out on a limb here, too. Apples often are shipped and stored with care and kept cool when on display. But we've all known the disappointment of biting into a mealy supermarket apple, its skin promising what the flesh can no longer deliver.

The shopper's first rule of thumb is that looks are deceiving. Some newly introduced apples, such as Fuji and Mutsu, are humble in appearance when placed next to a pile of shiny Macs or Red Delicious, but superior in taste.

From 20 to 30 percent of Red Delicious, the American best seller, will be in poor shape by the time they're purchased, according to one estimate. The flesh of an apple that is past its prime will have softened to a mealy mush and may look watery and translucent near the core. The characteristic flavor of the variety will have departed, and any tartness along with it. If that's all an apple delivers, within a day or two after purchase, you were sold damaged goods. Complain—and next time, ask for a sample.

3. EATING APPLES, SERIOUSLY

❖　　　❖　　　❖

Bite into an apple, and more than three hundred flavorful and aromatic molecules compete for your attention. Apple lovers have tried for years to lend some order to this sensual bath. Terms seem to help. So do informal taste tests, in which people communally search for words to describe the samples.

Traditionally apples have been categorized by their primary use. *Dessert* varieties are those best suited for eating fresh or "out of hand." *Culinary* varieties typically are harder and tarter and best enjoyed cooked down into sauce or baked. And *cider* varieties have their own standards, involving a range of qualities that contribute to a balanced beverage. These terms have fallen from popular use. Having lost our sophistication about apples (as well as our habits of baking and pressing cider), we rarely encounter anything but dessert apples.

JUST DESSERTS

Supermarket apples invariably are dessert apples. Where certain varieties once would have been specified for baking, sauce, and cider, dessert apples now stand in. Most serve capably enough. But we are missing the full spectrum of tastes and textures known to our ancestors.

Fortunately there are hundreds of dessert varieties to be tasted, and they offer many pleasures. Mail-order apple merchant Tom Vorbeck has come up with a simple two-class system to differentiate between them. There are connoisseur apples, including those high-flavored varieties you might declare your favorite yet not desire a steady diet of. Ashmead's Kernel, Golden Russet, Tydeman's Late Orange, and Freyberg fall into this group. And there are all the rest, the "everyday" apples, including such mild-mannered (but not necessarily bland) fruit as Gala and Melrose.

WHAT'S IN AN APPLE?

An average-size apple, weighing in at about 5½ ounces, delivers the following:

Calories	80
Carbohydrates	18 grams
Protein	0.3 grams
Fat	0.5 grams
Dietary fiber	5 grams
Cholesterol	0
Sodium	0
Potassium	170 milligrams

Recent years have seen a rash of taste tests across the United States and Canada. This has to do with the urgency people feel about rescuing old varieties and identifying the best of the new. It also may testify to our insecurity over just what makes a good apple. If these rankings tell us anything, it's that humans vary greatly in what they consider the ideal.

Each of us has his or her idiosyncrasies, of course. There are taste differences between cultures as well. Comparing surveys from several parts of the world, you can see that Europeans tend to give top marks to high-flavored sweet-tart varieties (those with considerable sweetness *and* tartness). In America our preference is for a somewhat sweeter, milder apple that's cold and delivers a good crunch. Tasters from Asia and the Middle East favor very sweet apples. (The Japanese will leave fruit on the tree until past ripe—in fact, until the center turns syrupy with the condition Westerners call water core damage.)

CONDUCTING A TEST OF YOUR OWN

No one needs to be told how to eat an apple. But an organized test, whether for yourself or a couple of dozen friends, will bring all the senses to bear on the delicate business of *savoring* an apple. People who really love apples, and regard each harvest as a reunion with old friends, speak of the feel of the fruit in the hand, the particular sound the flesh makes as it is bitten into, and nuances of taste and smell that are as wildly impressionistic as an oenophile's.

You can share an apple by passing it from person to person, of course, but apple aficionados like to cut out wedges with sharp pocketknives. It's best that testers be armed with their own knives, slicing as they go, so that the samples don't have time to turn brown. (Browning, by the way, marks an apple's defense against dehydration and disease. As the flesh is cut, ruptured compartments spill a disinfectant that kills disease organisms. Other cells form a taut membrane across the wound.)

The apples should not be peeled. In certain varieties much of the flavor and aroma is concentrated in the peel. You might plan on offering water and bread, salt-free pretzels, or crackers, both to clear the palate between samples and to buffer the effect of a lot of apple in the stomach. With a few exceptions, apples whisper their distinctive qualities, and wine and sharply flavored foods can steal the show.

Not all apple experts dissect the objects of their affection. For himself, Tom Vorbeck prefers a full frontal assault: You shine the apple on your shirt, and then you tuck into it.

4. APPLES IN THE KITCHEN

❖   ❖   ❖

Mrs. Rowe's Kitchen, a roadside restaurant that has served Virginia's Shenandoah Valley since 1947, offers fried green apples among the traditional items on its breakfast menu. What variety does it use?

"Green apples," said a waitress not long ago.

But what kind of green apples?

"Green apples from a can."

Apples have lost their once-famous reputations for specific kitchen talents. *The Fannie Farmer Cookbook* formerly specified Porter apples for a pie recipe, but that old variety is now almost impossible to find. Using a single variety for pies, baking, cooking, cider, and eating fresh, as we have come to do, would have been as inappropriate as using mozzarella cheese for fondue and salad dressing.

Culinary apples tend to be tart. Heat reduces acidity, and a mild-mannered variety runs the risk of cooking into a bore. Also, the acid in a tart apple helps break down the cell walls and soften the flesh. That's an advantage when making a sauce. But if you are constructing a pie, a variety that collapses will leave a steamy amphitheater below the crust.

When apple flesh is exposed to air, chemical changes take place that turn the surface brown. To preserve the apple's whiteness for fruit salads, dip it first in a bowl of lemon juice. Or use one of the few varieties that stay conspicuously white, such as Cortland.

As for flavor, you want a lot of it going into a recipe because it tends to be driven off by heat. Many recipes call for sugar. It doesn't counteract the acidity—sour is sour—but sweetness can blunt a tart edge and give a balanced taste. Keep in mind that sweeteners, measured with a heavy hand, also tend to mask the characteristic flavors of an apple. Some cooks incorporate sweeter varieties with their sauces and pies in order to cut down on added sweetener.

DRYING

Until refrigeration came along, drying was the human species' principal defense against rot. Apples were routinely dried each fall to ensure a supply of fruit year-round. Farms often had small dryhouses devoted to dehydrating produce for storage. A dryhouse looks like a smokehouse, which looks like an outhouse. Screen-bottomed drawers of food slide into the front of the structure and are speedily dehydrated by the heat of a wood fire within.

VARIETIES FOR DRYING

Sweet	Tart
Black Gilliflower	*Cortland*
Criterion	*Winesap*
Gala	
Grimes Golden	
Maiden Blush	
Paradise	
Summer Rambo	
Wolf River	

Dried apples are not only practical but a distinct treat in themselves. They make a healthful snacking alternative to potato chips and also figure in old recipes. Schnitz, the Pennsylvania German term for dried apple, is used in schnitz und knepp, a dumpling stew with enough ham for flavor. Sweet apples are used, dried with the skins on so that the slices will hold up. Peeled tart schnitz is preferred for out-of-season apple pies.

SCHNITZ

If the schnitz is to be used in a stew, leave the peels on. Otherwise, peel good drying apples, cut them in eighths, and spread on grills laid over the racks of the oven. Place a clothespin in the door to let moisture escape, and dry at 225 degrees for up to twelve hours, checking the apples from time to time. They should be somewhat pliable, but not at all mushy.

Tuck the schnitz away in bags of cloth or perforated plastic to allow some ventilation.

APPLE LEATHER

Another form of dried apple is fruit leather. It's easy to make and is free of the added sugar typical of the commercial product.

18 apples of a good drying variety
2 cups sweet cider
Spices to taste, optional (ground cinnamon, clove,
coriander, allspice, or nutmeg)

Peel and core the apples, and then mash them with a food mill or blender. Pour the fruit into a pot, add the cider and spices, and cook. Stir frequently until the fruit has thickened to the consistency of runny jam. Lightly oil four standard-size cookie sheets with edges. Remove the fruit from the stove, and pour it onto the sheets to an even depth of one-quarter inch or so.

To dry the fruit into a pliable leather, you have a few options: Place it, protected with cheesecloth, in a sunny, warm location; set it atop a woodstove; or bake it in an oven set low, with the door slightly ajar. Check the consistency often. To store the finished product, dust it lightly with corn-starch when cool, place a sheet of wax paper over the fruit, and roll it up.

APPLESAUCE

Walda Janson, who with her husband, Fred, grows many varieties at their home near Rockton, Ontario, has made applesauce from a hundred varieties. But a Pennsylvania orchardist, Marguerite Hobert, likes the counterpoint of just two varieties, Cortland and Jonathan. A simple sauce lets a couple of voices sing; a complex blend makes an intriguing symphony to eat meditatively.

VARIETIES FOR SAUCE

Braeburn	*King David*
Calville Blanc	*Newtown Pippin*
Gala	*Pink Pearl*
Golden Delicious	*Tolman Sweet*
Granny Smith	*Wagener*
Haralson	*Wealthy*
Jonagold	*Winesap*
Jonathan	*Yellow Bellflower*

Many ways have been found to render a hard, round apple into a puree. The consistency of the final product is a matter of personal taste. Should the results be chunky or velvety smooth? With skins (they hold most of the flavor and aroma of certain varieties) or without? And will you add flavorings and sugar or go it straight? The choices are yours. Here is a basic recipe.

8 to 10 apples

¾ cup cider or water

You can select varieties known as sauce apples, but most apples will do. For balance, try combining a sweet variety with a tart apple.

Wash, peel, quarter, and core the apples. Add a smidgen of grated quince for its aroma, if you care to. Leave out the sugar and cinnamon for now, and let the fruit do the work.

Place the apples in a heavy-bottomed saucepan, add an inch of the cider or water, and simmer until tender, adding more liquid as necessary. Use a whisk or a blender to reduce the lumps.

Give the sauce a taste. Add sweetener, if necessary, and return the pan to the stove for a few minutes. Taste the sauce once more; if it seems bland, stir in fresh lemon juice, and remove from the heat.

Unlike applesauce, this thick spread undergoes a long, slow cooking that caramelizes the sugar in the fruit, turning it brown and giving it a mellow flavor.

In some regions, apple butter is made with apples alone, but the typical Pennsylvania German recipe calls for more cider than fruit. Although Fallawater, Idared, and Wolf River are noted apple butter varieties, you can try any apple recommended for sauce.

Apples
1 gallon cider per pound of apples

Peel, core, and dice the apples, and partly cover them with preservative-free cider in a heavy saucepan. Simmer over low heat, adding cider as necessary to keep the butter bubbling and safe from scorching. Cooking time depends on the juiciness of the apples you use; allow four hours to develop full flavor.

APPLE RULES OF THUMB

For a pound of apples, select four small apples, three medium apples, or two large apples.

Plan on using roughly two pounds of apples for a nine-inch pie.

One pound of apples yields about three cups when diced.

There is no recipe here for this American standard. Most households have their favorite version.

We think of apple pie as a dessert, but in the past it has served as a basic food. For families on hardscrabble farms in the Northeast, suppers through the winter might consist of nothing but apple pie and milk, day after day.

VARIETIES FOR PIE

Bramley's Seedling	*Newtown Pippin*
Calville Blanc	*Northern Spy*
Cox's Orange Pippin	*Northwestern Greening*
Granny Smith	*Rhode Island Greening*
Grimes Golden	*Spigold*
Holstein	*Summer Rambo*
Idared	*Wealthy*
Jonagold	*Yellow Bellflower*
Jonathan	*York Imperial*
Macoun	

We also have come to think of pie apples as big and green, but that, too, is a limited view. A good pie apple should have three characteristics, and size and greenness aren't among them. A degree of tartness is important if the fruit is to stand up to the oven's heat and the recipe's sweetener. Second, slices should keep their shape and not dematerialize into sauce. Finally, a durable, aromatic flavor is vital, unless your recipe leans heavily on lemons and cinnamon. (Lemons and cinnamon, as readers of Ritz cracker boxes know, can be used to mimic an apple pie with no apples whatsoever.)

5. THE HARD AND SOFT OF CIDER

❖ ❖ ❖

Grind up a few apples, express their juice, and a minor miracle of alchemy takes place. That clear, lifeless, sugary liquid changes immediately to a cloudy brew that, left to its own devices, will pitch itself into a fizzing tempest. The end product is a complex and stable beverage, mildly alcoholic, with an agreeable bitterness. It was once the most popular beverage in America, serving in the place of water, milk, wine, and hard liquor in households and taverns.

The drink was called cider, and it has all but vanished from the United States and Canada. The reasons have to do with the nature of cider itself: quick to ferment, easy to manufacture. Its great popularity helped incite a wave of temperance sentiment in the 1800s.

Temperance not only did away with the drink but also bowdlerized the name. The stuff we now call cider would have been called juice; cider was the juice after undergoing the spontaneous fermentation that seizes it—unless chemical preservatives are added, as is usually the case today. Most states and provinces now require cider to be clinically dead if the producer expects to hold on to it for more than a day or two.

Ralph Waldo Emerson called the apple the "social fruit of New England." He was referring to cider—the fermented version—and his remark held for any part of America that grew apples.

The English brought the cider habit with them to America. Since medieval times they had looked upon apples as a source of beverage, rather than as something to eat. So it was no great loss when English colonists found that grapevines from home wouldn't flourish here. They turned instead to the apple. A family that wanted a tract of Virginia land was required to plant an orchard before claiming ownership.

Cider was regarded as a healthful beverage, to be served at every meal. Accounts of Pennsylvania farm life in the 1700s say that families typically put up fifteen to forty barrels of cider each fall, often choosing a horse with a placid disposition to power the fruit grinder. Children drank it cut with water. Adults enjoyed it in curious-sounding beverages that have been long forgotten. A syrupy drink called mole-cider was made by stirring in milk and beaten egg. Cider soup was thickened with flour and sweet cream and sprinkled with croutons. Although cider was usually prepared without flavorings, sweetener might be added to increase the alcoholic content and prolong shelf life. Cider was so highly valued that recipes circulated for making it artificially, combining such ingredients as yeast, honey, tannic acid, alum, almonds, cloves, and caramel, with a touch of cider vinegar for tartness.

Fully fermented cider was distilled to make apple brandy, a concentrated drink that could be stored and shipped more easily. New Jersey sent more than its share through the coils, and in 1810 a local orchardist reported that Essex County alone had distilled 307,310 gallons of apple brandy. But the cider and brandy boom would not continue much longer.

CIDER GOES SOFT

As teetotalers inveighed against alcohol, their campaign extended to the apple as well. Orchards were toppled across the countryside: tens of thousands of trees. The fruit of fable and allegory had come to be regarded as a drug factory.

By the time the temperance movement had spent itself, most distillers had switched from apples to grains. Beer, another grain beverage, became the carbonated drink of choice. Cartoonists used the cider barrel as a symbol of back-woods Americana, and by 1900 the term *cider* had been stripped of its original meaning. In North America, that is.

Great Britain was unruffled by the temperance movement; cider remained cider, and juice was still juice. Cider continues to be widely available there on tap, and old cider varieties, such as Chisel Jersey, Ellis Bitter, and Ashton Bitter, are still grown for their quirky flavor.

WHAT MAKES A GOOD CIDER APPLE?

Traditionally cider was carefully orchestrated with a selection of apple varieties, classified as sweets (low in both tannins and acidity); bittersweets (high in tannins, low in acidity); bitter-sharps (high in both tannins and acidity); and sharps (low in tannins, high in acidity). Today, however, most American cider is pressed from any apple that rolls along. We simply describe cider apples as either sweet or tart, if we bother to classify them at all.

CIDER APPLES

Sweet	Tart
Baldwin	Winesap
Red Delicious	Jonathan
Golden Delicious	Stayman
Cortland	York Imperial
Rome	Newtown Pippin
Empire	Macoun
Grimes Golden	Northern Spy
Tolman Sweet	Rhode Island Greening
Fameuse	Wealthy
Golden Russet	McIntosh

Good commercial mills continue to mind their blends. A variety becomes sweeter over its harvest period, and knowledgeable ciderists will make adjustments as the weeks go by. At Chittenden's Cider Mill, near Burlington, Vermont, Macs are the mainstay, but sweet varieties have to be added early in the season to offset the young Macs' tartness. Thompson's Cider Mill, in New York's lower Hudson Valley, typically combines between five and thirteen varieties, with Golden Russet the star apple.

PUTTING UP CIDER

Cider can be stored for an extended period if kept just over 32 degrees Fahrenheit. It will keep a year or more if frozen in plastic jugs; take out a cup of cider to allow for expansion.

But our mills aren't able to duplicate ciders of the past because key ingredients were lost when America abandoned its cider orchards. Harrison, the most popular variety in the cider hub of Newark, New Jersey, has disappeared. Campfield and Poveshon are lost as well. Graniwinkle, its juice syruplike in body and sweetness, still exists, but trees are sold by just two mail-order nurseries.

The easiest way to make your own preservative-free cider is with a countertop juicer. For more production, you have to move up to a cider press that will both grind the apples and forcefully squeeze the juice from the resulting pulp. Old cider presses are common but so cute that they've become collectibles. Several models continue to be made; see the listings under Sources, at the back of the book.

You'll find that not all cider looks alike. Certain varieties, such as Cortland, are slow to oxidize, and make a pale drink that may look watery unless they are part of a blend. Geneva, Dolgo, and other red-fleshed crab apples have been used commercially to make sparkling rosé ciders.

MAKING HARD CIDER

Each fall people continue to be accessories to cider's eager fermentation. So it has been for thousands of years. If you want to buy this distinctive drink, you'll have to travel to Europe or hunt down the cider introduced by Vermont's Joseph Cerneglia Winery. The company offers two types of its Woodchuck cider, both in bottles and on tap: Dark and Dry uses caramelized sugar for color and added flavor; Amber is a paler brew. The cider is pressed from regionally grown McIntosh apples, fermented to about the alcoholic content of domestic beer, and given a shot of added carbonation.

Fortunately, low-alcohol hard cider is the easiest of beverages to brew at home. Just loosen the cap of a plastic gallon jug of unpasteurized, preservative-free cider, allow it to sit in a cool place, and wait. It will soon reach the stage New England cider makers call "picky"—barely effervescent, with bubbles that tickle the tongue and a trace of alcohol. It's still a family drink. Allowed to gestate a little longer, the cider enters a second, more vigorous fermentation. The jug begins to hiss and buzz angrily, and cider and foam dribble over the top.

Traditional cider apples have a high sugar content and can yield as much as 6 percent alcohol, comparable to strong beer. But chances are your cider is made from run-of-the-mill apples, with less fermentable sugar. You may want to intervene at this point and make a headier brew by adding sweetener. Use a pound of light-flavored honey per gallon. To mix in the honey, heat it with roughly two parts of cider on the stove, and mix well. Stir this into the container, and place the jug in a spot that won't be damaged by the cider eruption you've just incited. Once a day stir the liquid both to distribute any honey that has settled to the bottom and to discourage sulfurous-smelling fermentation.

As long as the vigorous bubbling continues, keep the jug filled with fresh cider. You can remove the cap and tuck a wad of cotton in its place to keep out dirt and fruit flies. Sampled now, the cider will have an off-putting yeasty odor. Kids won't like it, and they shouldn't be served in any case.

As the bubbling subsides, add a good-size rubber balloon or an inexpensive plastic fermentation lock to exclude air. Apple solids and spent yeast now line the bottom, leaving a pale liquid above that tastes quite dry and winelike.

The little liquid storm eventually will exhaust itself, the yeast having used up the sugar—that is, if the recipe has proceeded according to script. Take a small sip; if the liquid is very sweet, the fermentation is "stuck" and needs a nudge to finish its work. Do this by moving the vessel to a warmer place or, should that fail, adding a commercial champagne yeast.

The cider is best enjoyed when it retains a bit of fizz. Drink it now, well chilled. Serve it straight or half-and-half with beer. To enjoy it through the winter, put some up in heavy champagne bottles. Residual sugar should continue to feed the yeast, naturally carbonating the cider, and bottles must be stored where they won't be a hazard or make an undue mess if they explode. Handle the bottles with caution, and open only when they are well chilled. Unless you use a hydrometer to gauge just how the fermentation is proceeding, you can't predict how much pressure will build up in the bottle.

Once you get the hang of making cider in gallon batches, you're ready to graduate to five-gallon carboys or used whiskey barrels. With the jump up in scale comes the delicious smell of a winery, along with every fruit fly within a mile.

Granny wine is the pejorative term for any wine not lucky enough to have been made from grapes. The implication is that other fruits produce sickly sweet wines that no one should take seriously.

Vermont's Joseph Cerneglia Winery, finding itself in a climate unfriendly to traditional wine grapes, takes its apple wine seriously. Several varietals are offered: Granny Smith, Northern Spy, Macoun, McIntosh, Golden Delicious, and Empire.

To make your own wine, follow the recipe for hard cider, and then let the second fermentation run its course until the liquid is completely still—that is, no longer bubbling. Don't expect the liquid to taste like wine at this stage. There will be the funky smell of yeast about it.

Once the liquid turns clear, siphon it off into clean bottles, being careful to avoid picking up the sediment. Cork the bottles; store them for six months or so; then refrigerate a bottle and have a taste. If the wine strikes you as raw and unformed, give it another six months.

This is a very simple recipe, and it has its risks. Just as sourdough starters vary from year to year and place to place, the organisms that affect wine cannot be counted on. By allowing them to run riot in your sweet medium, as was traditional practice, you're entering a speculative collaboration with nature. The results may be exceptionally fine. Or you may find your wine is the victim of an unfriendly take-over by bad organisms, resulting in an odor of burned rubber, a sherrylike quality, or a ropy consistency.

For winemaking to be a sure thing, you have to begin by killing everything in the fresh, unfermented cider. The conventional method is to add food preservative, such as a solution of sodium metabisulfite, to the freshly pressed juice, while fastidiously rinsing all vessels, spoons, caps, siphons, and funnels with the chemicals. The serendipity of wild yeast is nipped in its bud. You're left with an inactive liquid and have to recolonize it. Baker's yeast will set the cider to bubbling, but you should use champagne yeast, a specialized strain. Preservatives, yeast, and fermentation locks are available at beer and winemaking shops and through the mail-order sources listed in the Sources section.

BACK PORCH APPLEJACK

Once your honey-fortified cider has fermented, you can convert it to a sterner drink by enlisting another natural phenomenon, cold winter nights. For centuries, northerners have frozen much of the water out of hard cider. The result is known variously as frozen-heart applejack, cider oil, or Jersey lightning.

Having added sweetener to cider and fermented it fully, you fill plastic jugs within a few inches of the top and place them outside on a night when the temperature is headed toward zero. Early the next morning, before the temperature goes back up, pour off the liquid core within the ice. (You can drill down through the ice block to reach the core, or tap it with a hot poker.) On the next cold night set this refined liquid out in the same way. Again, pour off the liquid that remains. You'll have a rich, thick, potent drink that should keep well in the refrigerator.

How strong is this stuff? If the thermometer drops to five below, you might reach the potency of a strong wine; a cold snap of thirty below can yield a concentration of up to 33 percent alcohol, or 66 proof.

APPLE BRANDY

Apple brandy is a clear or golden beverage distilled from hard cider. It is also known domestically as applejack, as *eau de vie de pomme* or calvados in France, and as *Trebern* in Austria.

You can't distill your own; that's a heavily taxed enterprise under the jealous control of federal laws. And you may have trouble buying it because the once-flourishing apple brandy centers of New Jersey and Quebec were decimated by competition from grain beverages, as well as by Prohibition. But a few companies have kept alive the tradition of distilling hard cider.

Laird's, a family-owned New Jersey distillery since 1780, makes a seven-and-a-half-year-old apple brandy from a number of varieties as they appear on the market. Clear Creek Distillery of Portland, Oregon, distills a brandy from Golden Delicious that, after two years in French oak, tastes like fire but still breathes the unmistakable scent of the fresh fruit. Two Canadian-born varieties, McIntosh and Fameuse, dominate the brandy made by a Quebecois firm, Cidrobec.

6. THE ORCHARD

❖ ❖ ❖

Apples and humans have been intimates over countless generations of husbandry. By selecting seed, pollinating, and grafting, we have placed our hands on that species's evolution. The tiny, hard, green nuggets of an ancient apple, *Pyrus malus*, have multiplied into the thousand apples of commerce. Along the way the apple tree has become as domesticated as a pet dog, and just as dependent on us.

Until well into the 1800s most orchards were casual groves of trees grown from seed. Because an apple seed doesn't grow a replica of the parent, but only a rough facsimile, these orchards were full of individuals, each one a variety unto itself. But then grafting became common practice, and Thoreau lamented that seedling groves were giving way to the rigid rank and file of look-alike trees.

Look-alike trees were what the growers were after. They wanted to be able to reproduce valuable varieties. By grafting wood of a known variety onto the base of another tree, they could be confident that the limbs sprouting forth would be clonal replicas of that variety.

While growers rely on this vegetative, asexual style of reproduction, apple breeders are after variable results. They value the birds and the bees as the fruit's own R and D laboratory.

The exchange of pollen between blossoms creates a never-ending, never-duplicated string of experiments. For the apple tree this helps ensure survival in a changing world. For the breeder, there is the one in eighty thousand chance (by one estimate) that a seed will grow into a tree of commercial value.

The long odds can be improved if the breeder's finger, not a bee, does the pollinating. Bees impregnate blossoms with whatever pollen happens to be clinging to their chaps; the tree engineers these springtime blind dates, using the wiles of perfume, nectar, and the pale pinks of a negligee. That suits the tree and presumably the bee. But fruit scientists want to exercise as much control over pollination as possible.

They transfer the pollen from one known parent to the unopened blossoms of another variety. The blossoms are then emasculated with a sharp knife, removing both petals and sepals, to make them less attractive to bees with their random pollen. Of these blossoms, roughly half can be expected to bear fruit. Seed is gathered from the apples at the end of the season and planted the following spring.

And then comes the wait. It takes three to ten years for the seedlings to grow up and bear fruit—and the proof is in the fruit. Although these trees are offspring of the same parents, they will produce apples as variable as human children. Only 1 percent, on average, will be talented enough to pique the curiosity of the researchers. The rest are yanked out of the ground.

The chosen few are each given a number, grafted onto a rootstock to regulate their growth, and then judged over the next decade—sometimes over several decades. If a variety is made commercially available (or "introduced," something like a debutante's coming out), its number will be replaced with a name.

GROW YOUR OWN VARIETY

If you want to participate in the great genetic crap shoot, collect seeds from mature fruits, and refrigerate them in aluminum foil until early in the new year. Remove the seeds, place them in a dish filled with damp vermiculite or sphagnum moss, and refrigerate for four to six weeks. Then stick the seeds in pots and keep them watered. Transplant the seedlings to the yard, using screening to protect their tender bark from mice. And see what develops.

TAKING ADVANTAGE OF GOOD SPORTS

To orchardists, a sport is a gift from nature, a naturally occurring mutation on part of a tree. A limb may spontaneously produce fruit that tastes better, shows resistance to pests, or enjoys another advantage over the standard variety. A bit of this exceptional wood is then grafted onto a rootstock to perpetuate the strain.

It takes a sharp and knowing eye to spot a sport, and fortunes have been made from just a single branch. A recent case in point is Scarlet Gala, an extra-red sport of the normally quiet variety, found hanging from the branch of a tree in Kentucky.

GROWING YOUR OWN FRUIT

Even if you love to garden and love to eat apples, you may not love orcharding. Apples lean heavily on human help, and you have to be beetle-browed in your devotion to a backyard orchard, from March pruning through postharvest cleanup.

One bright note is that in spite of what you'll learn from books, extension pamphlets, and labels, you don't have to spray as religiously as a commercial orchardist. People who grow apples for their livings must produce a high percentage of good-looking fruits or go out of business. But you should be able to cull a good part of your crop, tossing the rejects in the compost pile, and still eat well on what's left over.

To improve your prospects, heed a few suggestions from nurseries that deal with small-scale growers. First, become a knowledgeable eater of apples. Sample them at local tastings and roadside stands. Ask orchardists to name their favorites. Identify the apples you really like, and then narrow your list to those you can't buy readily.

Next, scratch from your list those varieties that can't be expected to flourish on your site. Almost any apple tree will push out leaves, but the fruit may be sparse, ugly, or just plain insipid unless its growing requirements are met.

If you don't want to be wedded to a spraying schedule, investigate disease-resistant trees. Several are featured in this book, and new ones are under development. You can further spare yourself hours of work by choosing dwarfed trees, for ease in spraying, pruning, and picking. Dwarfs bear sooner after planting, too. Note that the *fruit* isn't smaller than standard; just the tree is, because the variety has been grafted onto a rootstock that limits its size.

Even if apples give you colic, the trees would be a worthwhile addition to your landscape. With their roots in the earth and their branches reaching for the closest star, they link our practical lives with the divine. The blossoms have an innocent one-note fragrance. And can you name a better climbing tree?

Apples

Akane

The fertilization lottery smiled upon this apple, a cross between the well-known Jonathan and the obscure Worcester Pearmain. It's pronounced ah-cahn-nuh and was introduced in Japan in 1970.

Akane comes highly recommended as a dessert apple, with an invigorating, tart taste and a marked aroma. Beneath its thin skin, the bright white flesh is juicy and crisp; your teeth know they've bitten into something.

If you leave the peels on, Akane will make a pinkish sauce with very good flavor; strain the sauce after cooking. Pie slices keep their shape. The apples can be dried successfully.

Akane is harvested over an extended period, from August through mid-September, and will not keep its quality for long in storage.

Arkansas Black

When it comes to naming apples, "black" is used with as much license as "blue" in flower names. But this reddish purple variety can, in fact, approach black at the end of the season. It is thought to be a seedling of Winesap, selected in Benton County, Arkansas, around 1870.

Beneath that attractive dark, waxy skin, the golden flesh is juicy, firm, and crisp, with a notable aroma. Arkansas Black lends itself to cider and is suited for cooking.

The apples are picked in October or November and gain in flavor in storage.

Arlet

Arlet is a promising variety. Its American marketing handle, Swiss Gourmet, makes the apple sound more like a perfumed coffee blend. But this is indeed a Swiss variety, spawned by two Americans, Golden Delicious and Idared.

The flesh is firm and pleasantly tart, rounded off with enough sweetness to make a fine dessert apple.

Arlet is harvested in September and can be refrigerated for two to three months. The skin becomes greasy in storage but can be rinsed off easily.

Ashmead's Kernel

The object shown here is a window on what apples were like three hundred years ago: short on shine but long on flavor. Ashmead's takes its name from the Gloucester, England, physician who grew it in the 1700s. A kernel is a fruit seed, or a tree grown from seed.

This apple is distinguished, and distinguishable, and that explains why it's riding the crest of a new interest in old varieties. The crisp yellow flesh is mouth-puckering just off the tree, becoming sweet, juicy, and pleasantly aromatic in the weeks following its September or October harvest. Even then Ashmead's is "not for sissy palates," warns Tom Vorbeck of Applesource, an Illinois mail-order apple company. The variety remains popular in England and came up fifth in a tally of apples grown by members of the Royal Horticultural Society's fruit group.

This is a good cider apple and a good one to store for winter eating.

Baldwin

Few American apples have risen so high in popularity and then sunk so low. Baldwin was our first true commercial variety. For a short period in the early 1900s it was the number one apple in the United States. But Baldwin ran into a shiny competitor from Canada—McIntosh—and was bumped from the marketplace.

When New England growers got together in the 1920s to concentrate their time and marketing dollars on just seven varieties, Baldwin made the cut, but only because it was seen as a sentimental favorite of the public. The variety's fortunes slipped further in the 1930s, when a severe winter knocked out nearly half the Baldwin trees in the Northeast.

Baldwin began as a seedling in the northeastern Massachusetts town of Wilmington, sometime before 1750. The apple was named for a Colonel Baldwin, who grafted trees from the original seedling. The site of that first tree is marked with a monument topped by a stone apple.

The thick, tearing skin is on the tough side. Baldwin's yellow flesh is crisp, coarse, and juicy, with a spicy character that recommends it as a cider apple and for pies.

Harvesttime varies between late September and November. The apples keep well.

Belle de Boskoop

The apple that came from below sea level, Belle de Boskoop is among the world's best-known russeted varieties and may be the only one still grown commercially. It was found in the 1850s near the town of Boskoop, Netherlands, between Amsterdam and Rotterdam, and it sailed to America a couple of decades later.

This variety looks as though it would have character, and it does. The firm, crisp flesh is a pale yellow-green in color, tart, somewhat dry, and highly flavored. In taste tests at Oregon State University most people complained Boskoop was sour and too strongly flavored. The somewhat timid American palate could be blamed for that, but in fact, Boskoop tends to be daunting until it has had a chance to mellow and sweeten after harvest.

Although Boskoop has never caught on here in the land of Red Delicious, it remains popular in its homeland and in Germany, both for eating fresh and for cooking.

The harvest varies from late September through December. Boskoop keeps well.

Ben Davis

Four southern states have been credited with bringing Ben Davis into the world. A hundred years ago that would have been something to brag about. This apple was the leading variety of the South and Midwest, and Virginia grower Tom Burford relates that it was called a mortgage lifter by growers who made a small killing in the export trade, floating barge-loads of Bens down the Mississippi to ships sailing from New Orleans.

But the affair with Ben Davis was a matter of convenience. The fruit grew abundantly and, having the toughness of a potato, could be shipped with little damage. The goods inside, however, weren't as impressive.

One bite reveals the white flesh (stained red below the chewy skin) to be dry, coarse, woolly, and unexceptional. Mail-order apple merchant Tom Vorbeck says of Ben Davis, "It keeps like a rock, but it's not a very good rock." Tom Burford isn't much more complimentary. He says, "They used to call it the cotton apple. Today, people are buying it for sheer nostalgia."

The crop ripens from late September into November and stores into the following year.

Black Gilliflower

Black Gilliflower can be summed up as tall, dark, and not particularly toothsome. This may be one antique apple that has survived by virtue of an interesting name (it's also quaintly called Sheepnose), shape (like a sheep's nose), and color (although "black" is in the tradition of horticultural hyperbole, the apple's deep red can be strikingly dark).

Black Gilliflower has been traced to Connecticut, sometime in the late 1700s. Its first flush of popularity had died out by the early 1900s, when it enjoyed a modest revival, and the old apple is again finding its way into nursery catalogs and apple tastings.

Beneath the dark skin the greenish flesh makes a marked contrast. Crisp it is not. The taste is rich and quite sweet, with an aroma of its own. Whatever its limitations as a dessert apple, Black Gilliflower gets good marks as a baker and has long been a traditional variety for drying.

The apples are ready for harvest in September or October. They store fairly well.

Blue Permain

Blue Permain is a New England variety, well known in that part of the country by the early 1800s. Before being buffed, the apples have a bluish bloom on their dark purplish skin. The fruit glows like plums against the tree's foliage, and orchard visitors are often stopped in their tracks by the sight.

Blue Permain is an interesting sight at close range as well. As if drawn on a windowpane by Jack Frost, the raised russeting may take the form of tiny daggers and scimitars, linked with a fine mesh.

This variety's waxy, somewhat tough skin yields to crisp, tender, fine-grained flesh. The flavor is rich and a bit tart. Orchardists describe the apple as "heavy in hand," meaning that it has a noticeably higher specific gravity than most. Blue Permain is a longtime favorite for cider.

The fruit is picked from late September through October and is not noted for keeping its quality in storage.

Braeburn

Braeburn is a chance seedling from New Zealand's South Island, introduced in 1952. That country, with its reverse seasons, ships Braeburns to reach our supermarkets in May and June. The variety is now being planted here but has met some resistance because it isn't as red as a fire engine. Nevertheless, Braeburn's tall shape and bright color are attractive in their own right.

Uncut, Braeburn may have a faintly cidery perfume. The skin is thin and seems to disappear in the mouth. The flesh is yellow-green to creamy yellow, breaking and crisp in texture. If the apples are harvested at the right time, they offer a complex, sweet-tart flavor, with a noticeably aromatic aftertaste— a match and then some for another popular newcomer, Fuji.

When cooked, Braeburn turns simpler but doesn't go flat. As sauce it needs little or nothing in the way of added sweetening, and in Australia the variety has been used to make applesauce for diabetics.

Braeburn ripens in October or November and stores well.

Bramley's Seedling

Two hundred years ago young Mary Anne Brailsford placed a pip in a pot. The seedling that sprouted forth came to be known as Bramley's Seedling, England's best baking apple. What is believed to be the original tree is growing still in a cottage garden on Church Street, Southwell, in Nottinghamshire. The apple received the name of a butcher who later took over the cottage. *Seedling* testifies that the tree was an accident of nature.

Eaten fresh Bramley's is firm, juicy, and piquantly acidic, and the tart juice (high in vitamin C) is a lively addition to cider blends. In recent years the variety has seen new interest in North America.

Apples are picked from October through early November. They keep well but over time will secrete a remarkably slick, greasy coat that can be rather unpleasant to the touch.

Calville Blanc

Here is an apple that sounds like a wine, smells like a banana, and has more vitamin C than an orange.

Nevertheless, Calville Blanc is not unpleasantly tart; the pale yellow flesh is tender and lively on the tongue. These qualities have made it the best-known dessert apple of France. Sharp-eyed grower Robert Nitschke has spotted Calville in Claude Monet's still life *Apples and Grapes*. The variety's marked shoulders and ridges give it away, he says.

Not many apples come with a consumer advisory, but Nitschke, writing in Southmeadow Fruit Gardens' catalog, warns that "Calville is not for the schoolboy's lunchbox." Its character serves it well in pies, sauce, cider, and cider vinegar. The apple has been cultivated since the 1500s and was grown by Thomas Jefferson, a devoted Francophile. Today Calville is among the most sought after of antique varieties.

Depending on climate and site, the apples are picked any time from late October to December. The color of Calville Blanc gets warmer in storage, as its flavor improves. If you like a crisp apple, don't put off eating it too long. And you needn't feel you're boorish if you don't detect the scent of bananas; experienced apple tasters admit failing to find a trace of it.

Chenango Strawberry

It doesn't look much like a strawberry. And some sources suggest the apple hails from Connecticut, not from its name-sake Chenango Valley in central New York State. No matter the accuracy of its name, Chenango Strawberry has been known since the mid-1800s. The variety is distinguished by its clear, shiny, see-through skin. The white flesh is tender, firm, slightly tart, and juicy, with an intense flavor and marked aroma that make Chenango a popular apple with backyard growers.

But because it is a delicate fruit, Chenango doesn't stand up well to the bruising bumps of shipping to market. Commercial growers have been further discouraged by its drawn-out harvest, from August through September, and its short storage life.

Cornish Gilliflower

Although this variety has been called an ugly duckling, it's more of a Cinderella. A close look shows Cornish Gilliflower to be a fascinating object, displaying subtle shifts in color and constellations sketched by the russeting. Its shape is curious as well, with ribs and a tapering base. The lore surrounding this variety puts its beginnings as a chance seedling by a house in Truro, out on England's Cornish peninsula, two centuries ago.

The yellow flesh is firm, fine-grained, and high-flavored. Written accounts claim an odor of cloves, and the name *gilliflower* long has been applied to describe plants, flowers especially, that have a clovelike scent. The term bounces back through time and various dialects to early French, Latin, and ancient Greek. But let your own senses be the judge.

The apples ripen in October and store fairly well.

Cortland

Cortland is a child of McIntosh and Ben Davis. It was an early success of the New York State Agricultural Experiment Station, which made the cross in 1898.

Cortland is larger than McIntosh, but Mac fans complain that Cortland has lost something of its parent's tang. The thin, tearing skin reveals crisp paper white flesh. The flavor is tart and tangy, but not emphatically so, and juicy to the point of messiness. In short, Cortland comes across as friendly; it's not a complex variety that will flood your sense gates, but it makes a good apple to accompany a sandwich. Or try it in pies and sauce. Cortland is suited for fruit salads because slices are unusually slow to brown when sliced. Finally, this rates as a good-tasting cider apple, although an all-Cortland cider is apt to look watery.

The harvest varies from September through early October. Apples lose market share just like corporations, and Cortland is being nudged by another New York State product, Empire.

Cox's Orange Pippin

At a romantic moment in A. S. Byatt's *Possession*, a contemporary novel that recently won Britain's coveted Booker Prize, our picnicking heroes pull out a couple of apples to munch while enjoying a view of the Yorkshire coast.

The variety? Granny Smith, discovered in Australia. If the book had been written a few decades earlier, chances are those fruits would have been Cox's Orange Pippins, the best-known dessert apple of the British Isles. But a survey found that Brits under thirty-five tend to prefer other varieties.

In the early 1800s Richard Cox, a retired brewery worker of Bucks, England, planted some Ribston Pippin seeds; one exceptional tree was given a name that coupled his own, the apple's unusual color, and an old term that signifies this is a dessert apple raised from seed. The original tree survived until blown down in 1905; the cottage continued to be a landmark for apple lovers until it was demolished in 1965.

This is a firm, juicy, full-flavored apple, with cream-colored flesh. Both an intriguing aroma and a balanced flavor set Cox's apart among fine dessert apples. It can be baked into a pear-scented pie and is a good cider ingredient.

Apples are ready to be picked from mid-September through mid-October and keep into January.

Criterion

Criterion was discovered as a chance seedling near Parker, Washington. The variety's genetic mix includes Red Delicious, Yellow Delicious, and Winter Banana. It was introduced in 1973.

The flesh is notably crisp, firm, and juicy. Criterion tastes mild and sweet, with a touch of tartness, and good aroma suffuses it all. This variety can be recommended for all kitchen uses, including drying.

Following the October harvest, the fruit will keep its quality for some months.

Elstar

Elstar is a distinctive-looking variety that finds fans among those who like to tangle with a tart apple. A cross of Golden Delicious and Ingrid Marie, it was developed in the Netherlands in the 1950s and introduced to America in 1972. Elstar does not do well in hot summers, which has limited its use in the United States, but the variety has become popular in Europe.

The cream-colored flesh is crisp and invites comparison with Jonagold. As well as being excellent eaten fresh, Elstar performs in recipes.

Harvest varies from August to October. The apple's sharp edge is moderated with a few weeks of storage.

Empire

This cross between the best-selling red varieties Red Delicious and McIntosh is the work of New York's Geneva Experiment Station. It was introduced in 1966 and has proved superior to the parent it most resembles, Mac, in redness, flavor, and post-harvest life. Not surprisingly, Empire has caught on with both growers and the apple-eating public.

But it's still not red enough in some eyes. The Temple Brothers discovered supersanguine Empires growing on a limb in its Wolcott, New York, orchard, and the added 15 percent of color earned an extra-fancy grade, as well as a new name, Royal Empire.

The creamy white flesh is crisp and juicy. Right off the tree, Empire is an excellent choice for eating out of hand if you like a loud, snapping apple that's sweeter than it is tart. Empires are frequently added to cider blends and can be used for cooking.

Harvest is in September or October. In storage the apples keep their quality well. There's an aesthetic harvest each spring, when the unusually pink blossoms appear.

Esopus Spitzenburg

Apple names ain't what they used to be. Among such upstarts as Red Sumbo and Deli-Jon, this grand old American variety sounds venerable, even wise. It was the favorite apple of Thomas Jefferson, who grew Spitzenburgs at Monticello·

The variety was found in the late 1700s on a farm near Esopus, a town in New York's Hudson Valley. Downriver, at Washington Irving's restored home, Sunnyside, a couple of gnarled Spitzenburgs are thought to have produced fruit for the author's table.

The flesh is pale yellow, firm, crisp, and tender, with an aromatic, spicy character. It ranks among the best dessert apples and is suited for baking.

Spitzenburg ripens in September or October and improves after picking. The fruit keeps well.

Fallawater

Although Fallawater was first recorded in the 1800s, growing on farms in Bucks County, Pennsylvania, its origin may date well before that. The apple's unusual name is thought to have been taken from the region's Tulpehocken tribe of Native Americans. Fallawater's generous size could be the inspiration behind another traditional name, Mollywopper.

Fallawater continued to be planted while other regional favorites—Evening Party, Ewalt, Hiester, Klaproth, Susan's Spice, Water, Winter Spice—vanished from the Pennsylvania landscape. The variety was valued enough that Pennsylvania Germans carried trees south as they migrated along the Appalachians into Virginia and North Carolina. Southern-grown Fallawaters seem to be a greener strain, on average, than apples in the North.

The apple is good eaten out of hand (or hands, if a young child is holding on) but deserves particular mention for pies, sauce, and apple butters. Its flesh is coarse and crisp. The flavor is mildly sweet, unassertive, and straightforward.

Look for the apples at roadside stands anytime from August to November. And you'll have to look; Fallawater is seldom grown commercially.

Fameuse

An exceptionally beautiful apple, although modest in size, Fameuse was offered to children as a Christmas stocking stuffer in simpler times. The skin often shows curious photo-like impressions where leaves and stems have blocked the sun. For maximum color, growers may take the trouble to trim leaves around some of the fruit.

The glistening snow white flesh inspired another popular name, Snow Apple; it may be stained reddish near the skin. Fameuse is unusually tender and juicy and possessed of a distinctively cidery, spicy flavor. It is the chosen cider ingredient at Chittenden's Cider Mill in Burlington, Vermont. The variety came to Vermont from Canada, where it is thought to have been grown from French seeds as early as the 1600s (*fameus* is Old French for "famous").

Fameuse is unusual in that its seeds tend to produce trees much like the parent. This measure of predictability has made Fameuse a good choice for breeding new varieties, and it may be a parent of a famous star, McIntosh.

The apples are ready to be picked in September and do not keep particularly well.

Fireside

Fireside is one of McIntosh's many descendants. It was crossed with Longfield and introduced by the Minnesota Agricultural Experiment Station in 1943. The apple finds use in the North, where it withstands extremely low temperatures. Look for a characteristic peening on the skin, as if the fruit had received thousands of taps from a tiny hammer.

The skin is rather chewy. The yellow-green flesh straddles the teeter-totter of sweet and sour; although mild in taste, it carries a suggestion of pears and can be richer in flavor and texture than McIntosh. The trade-off is a greener skin, but this is by no means an ugly apple, with its Christmasy contrast of colors. Fireside finds use in salads and baking.

Harvesttime is September or October. The apples keep exceptionally well.

Freyberg

Like Pernod, the French aperitif, Freyberg is chartreuse in color and tastes of licorice. As you sample it for that essence, see if you can detect other nuances that Freyberg fans have reported, such as fruit brandy, cinnamon, peach, lemon, rue, and cedar. Hints of pear and banana may haunt its juice.

The apple was developed in 1934 by J. H. Kidd, the man who brought us the better-known Gala and an earlier success, Kidd's Orange Red. The work was carried out at Greytown, New Zealand, northeast of Wellington, and the apple's name commemorates a New Zealand governor. Freyberg is a cross between Golden Delicious and Cox's Orange Pippin. The flesh is juicy and aromatic, creamy white in color, and fine-textured, with the intriguing complexity of Cox's. Freyberg can be used in the kitchen and the cider mill.

Apples are ready to pick from September through October. Their appearance suffers in storage, but the flavor remains intriguing.

Fuji

Fuji is one of the new international successes in pomology. Not a particularly gorgeous variety, it signals the reemergence of taste and texture as the main reasons for growing an apple.

Fuji was developed from American parents, Ralls Janet and Red Delicious, and its roots go deep into American history. It's said that Ralls Janet was named in 1793 by Thomas Jefferson as an honor to a French minister to the United States, Edmond Charles Genêt, and Caleb Ralls, a Virginia orchardist. Genêt gave a bit of budding wood to Jefferson, the story goes, who relayed it to Ralls.

Having become the most popular apple in both Japan and China, Fuji is spreading to sites in the United States that have sufficiently long growing seasons. The cream-colored, firm, fine-grained flesh seems something special from the first bite, as it fills the mouth with sweetness and juice. In taste tests Fuji consistently scores at or near the top, and among late-maturing varieties it is a standout.

The crop is ready for harvest from September through early November. Fuji is regarded as the best keeper of any sweet variety, and the apples retain their toothsome firmness for up to a year if refrigerated. You can even display this one in a fruit bowl for a few weeks without endangering its quality.

Gala

Gala is a strikingly attractive apple. The bright yellow skin is finely stippled with red, as if airbrushed, and the result is a near-neon intensity. From across a room you'd think you were looking at a peach. Gala was developed in New Zealand by J. H. Kidd, crossing Golden Delicious and his own Kidd's Orange Red. The work was done in the 1920s, but the apple wasn't named and introduced until the 1960s.

The pale, creamy yellow flesh is crisp and dense, with a mild, sweet flavor and good aroma. The fruit is not large, and especially small Galas are cleverly marketed here as lunchbox size. In taste tests Gala easily outscores McIntosh and is considered more sprightly than Golden Delicious. Tom Vorbeck of Applesource says that a typical first comment of people biting into one is "Best apple I ever had in my life." When cooked, Gala strikes some people as bland, but it can be dried with good results. Gala is also used in cider blends.

Fruits imported from New Zealand first appear in stores from August and on into October; your refrigerator will stretch the life of the apples another three or four months.

Golden Delicious

Golden Delicious is not related to the red variety of that name, although both were christened by Stark Brothers. This is a very easy apple to like. The skin is thin; the flesh, firm and crisp and juicy. Flavor and aroma are unmistakable, without being particularly assertive. Even the shape is somehow agreeable: large, tall, and conical. Golden Delicious strikes some cooks as too timid for the kitchen, but it can be used for pies and sauce with little or no sugar. Its distinctive aroma carries over into cider.

Golden Delicious began as a chance seedling, perhaps of Grimes Golden, on a farmer's hillside near Bomont, West Virginia. In 1914 Stark bought the tree for five thousand dollars, and protected its investment with a tall cage, complete with burglar alarm.

Apples ripen from mid-September through late October. The skin color can be a clue to quality; look for fruits that are pale yellow, not the chartreuse of an apple picked prematurely or the darker yellow that signals overripeness. The skin is quick to shrivel if the apples are at room temperature, but Golden Delicious should keep well if refrigerated in the crisper or a plastic bag.

Golden Russet

Of all old-time sweet apples for cider, this variety was mentioned most often. It continues to be the ingredient of choice at Thompson's Cider Mill near Croton-on-Hudson, New York.

Golden Russet is an early American apple, believed to have sprouted from a seed of English Russet. It was a commercially marketed variety by the early 1800s and won a following that rated it above a similar American apple, Roxbury Russet.

The yellow flesh is crisp, fine-textured, and brightly flavorful, with a notable sweetness that made it a traditional favorite for hard cider. The apples can be used for cooking and drying.

Harvest is in October. As with most russets, the apples keep well, but they need humid storage if they aren't to get soft under the skin.

GoldRush

GoldRush delivers one of the most stimulating experiences to be found on a tree. The 1992 Purdue introduction is a cross between Golden Delicious and an experimental apple. Don't be put off if the skin shows some fine russeting; that's part of the packaging, not a flaw.

The skin *can* be somewhat tough and chewy. The green-flecked gold flesh is extremely firm, breaking, and juicy. GoldRush has a tart, winy, clean edge that feels effervescent on the tongue, with just enough sweetness to keep the apple from being too aggressive. You might notice suggestions of other fruit flavors as well.

GoldRush is picked from October into November and rates as a very good keeper. Its color warms to gold in the months after harvest. On into the new year, the flesh remains remarkably crisp and firm, with a tart juiciness that will make you wish you'd stashed away a bushel.

Granny Smith

Granny Smith introduced American supermarket shoppers to the green apple. For a culture that had become unfamiliar with apples of that color, it came as a surprise that green does not necessarily mean unripe. Tart, Granny tends to be, but not sour and starchy.

The story goes that the first Granny Smith sprouted from a pile of apples tossed out by a southeast Australian named Mrs. Smith, back in 1868. This variety has succeeded commercially where other greens have not, for a few reasons. It is large. It is mild-flavored and has a good balance of tart and sweet. It is nearly as resilient as a tennis ball and holds up well in shipping. And Granny Smith will tolerate a half year of cold storage.

Brands of Granny applesauce and Granny apple juice are widely marketed. The apple can be baked as well. But eaten fresh, Granny is not an apple people tend to take to their hearts and name as their lifelong favorite. It's two-dimensional, lacking the hard-to-name qualities that make a fruit memorable.

The apples are harvested in October. As you sort through the piles of green fruits, keep in mind that paler Grannys, with a warmish cast, tend to be sweetest.

Gravenstein

Gravenstein has wandered around much of the world on its way to America. It is thought to have originated in either Russia or Italy, before becoming established in Schleswig-Holstein, the neck of land that has been on both sides of the German-Danish border. So you may find the apple referred to as Russian, Italian, German, or Danish. Whatever its itinerary, the variety arrived in the United States in the late 1700s and continues to be grown commercially in California.

Gravenstein is thin-skinned and juicy, with sweetness and enough acid to make it interesting. It is an outstanding summer apple and an orchard antique deserving of its renewed interest. The Gravenstein personality carries through when cooked in pies and sauce and is noticeable in an all-Gravenstein cider.

The fruit is picked in late July and August. Be wary of Gravensteins still on the market in fall; their quality doesn't hold up in storage, and fruits may have become soft and mealy.

Grimes Golden

Grimes is West Virginia's best-known gift to pomology. It was discovered in Brooke County in 1804 and named for the man who selected it, Thomas Grimes. Golden Delicious, one of the world's principal varieties, is thought to be a seedling of Grimes. You can see a family resemblance, but Grimes tends to be a richer golden green than its offspring.

Uncut, the apple is sharply perfumy. The flesh is a light cream color, tending toward an orangish tinge in some fruit. Grimes tastes rich and mildly spicy if the apples are grown well, with an unusual aroma of coriander. The texture is softer than Golden Delicious and does not produce the same snap when bitten into.

Grimes may not enjoy the huge international following of Golden Delicious, but some experienced growers name it as their favorite dessert apple. In Virginia's Blue Ridge Mountains, Grimes's high sugar content was put to good use in brewing hard cider. It is a good sauce constituent and pie variety, but don't expect it to hold up as a baked apple. Grimes can be stored by drying and freezing.

The apples ripen from late September into October and will keep through Christmas.

Haralson

This seedling of Malinda was grown at the University of Minnesota and introduced in 1923. Its breeders were after a hardy apple, and Haralson has proved popular with northern growers.

The white flesh is mild-tasting, somewhat tart, crisp, juicy, and tender. See if you note the scent of pineapple or lime. Haralson can be recommended for eating fresh, making cider, and baking (it doesn't collapse in the oven).

Harvest ranges from September to October. The apples should be good for another few months in storage.

Hawaii

Descriptions of a variety's flavor are passed between writers as readily as pinkeye, to become part of that fruit's lore. A scent of pineapple or banana has been repeatedly claimed for Hawaii, but you may find the most tropical thing about this apple is its name.

Even the name is misleading. Hawaii was developed in California in the 1940s, a cross between Golden Delicious (of West Virginia) and Gravenstein (a European). It can be said without equivocation that the yellow flesh is firm and juicy and quite pleasant.

The apples are picked in September. They store well but bruise easily.

Holstein

Holstein is one of several internationally known apples that owe a debt to Cox's Orange Pippin. It is a seedling of that variety, spotted in the Holstein region of Germany, near Hamburg, around 1918.

Holstein tends to be larger than Cox's. The yellowish white flesh is firm, somewhat coarse, sweet, and juicy. The nose will pick up the characteristic aroma of Cox's, but Holstein has an edge of tartness and a personality of its own. Try it in pies.

The crop ripens in late September and keeps well.

Honeygold

For short-season growers in the North Central states, Honeygold is a hardy alternative to Golden Delicious. It is a cross of that variety and Haralson, introduced in 1969 by Minnesota's Horticultural Research Center in Excelsior.

The flavor is quite sweet and may be missing some of the character of Golden Delicious. Honeygold ripens in October and stores very well.

Hubbardston Nonesuch

"Nonesuch" has been attached to highly esteemed apples since the 1700s. Going back nearly that far, this variety was the pride of Hubbardston, a small town in central Massachusetts.

Hubbardston Nonesuch has a great deal of personality, as something both to look at and to eat. With its hammered, multicolored surface and russeting, it is a handsomely aging character actor among apples. There is a monumentality about the fruit.

The hard, crisp, fine-grained flesh is complex, sweet, and highly flavored just after the October harvest. The fruit is tamed a bit by a few weeks in the refrigerator. There is a lot of eating in each apple because its core is small. A considerable sugar content made Hubbardston a popular hard cider variety.

Hudson's Golden Gem

With its heavy russeting and dull skin, this lopsided fruit is something only an apple lover could associate with a gem. Hudson's was discovered as a chance fencerow seedling at Hudson Nurseries in Tangent, Oregon. The variety was introduced in 1931 and is a good choice for backyard growers.

Hudson's might be confused with a pear in a blind tasting. The skin is dry and rough, and the sweet, juicy, grainy flesh tastes something like that of a pear.

Apples ripen toward the end of September and into October and keep their quality for up to three months.

Hyslop Crab

Hyslop (pronounced HISS-lup) is an old crab apple of obscure origins, first noted in America in 1869.

The flesh is yellow and relatively mild, but still too astringent to enjoy off the tree. Hyslop lends itself to making jelly. Virginia grower Tom Burford says his mother, in her nineties, insists that Hyslops be set aside each year so that she can put them up as pickles. Tom himself presses and freezes the juice to use as a piquant blending ingredient through cider season.

The apples are harvested in August or September. Hyslop isn't a variety to hang on to. Process it before the flesh becomes dry and characterless. The trees are attractive, with their olive-colored bark, serrated leaves, and fruit covered with a bluish bloom. Landscape architects put them to good use.

Idared

With its thick, handsome lipstick red skin, Idared is a commercial grower's idea of an apple, and it was developed with those growers in mind by the Idaho Agricultural Experiment Station. This cross of Jonathan and Wagener was introduced in 1942. Despite the apple's origin, most plantings are in the East and Midwest.

Uncut, Idared breathes a sweet perfume. The crisp pale yellow-green flesh is juicy, fine-grained, tender, a bit tart, and aromatic, with a taste something like Jonathan. Compared with other late-maturing varieties, Idared has not scored on top as a dessert apple. But it keeps its shape and flavor particularly well in pies, cooks down into a nicely colored sauce (leave the peels on and then strain), and is often used in apple butter.

The apples are ready to be picked from late September through late October. They gradually lose their tartness and character in storage.

Jonagold

The fortunes of Jonagold reveal much about national differences in apple appreciation. Although released in 1968 by New York State's Geneva Station, this cross of Jonathan and Golden Delicious has succeeded far better in Europe than at home. Large plantings have been made in Britain, France, Italy, Switzerland, and Belgium—Jonagold may become Europe's number one apple—as well as in Japan. But the home crowd resists it, preferring the familiar red, sweet, tame Red Delicious. It has been said that Americans eat apples with their eyes, and Jonagold is a case in point.

Nevertheless, this variety is the leading apple west of the Cascades in Washington State, and in British Columbia Jonagold challenges McIntosh as the number one variety.

With its aroma of Golden Delicious and the sprightliness of Jonathan, Jonagold is an excellent sweet-tart dessert apple. The texture of the creamy yellow flesh is noticeably crisp and juicy. In a poll of nineteen apple experts in nine countries, Jonagold scored as the overall favorite. The fruit makes fair sauce and a good pie.

Harvest varies from mid-September to late October. The apples keep well unless picked late in their two-week harvest period.

Jonalicious

In spite of its suggestive name, Jonalicious is of unknown parents. It ranks among the most popular apples at the tart end of the flavor spectrum and is a good variety for baking and cider, as well as for eating fresh.

But the tree is a shy bearer—there just aren't many there for the picking—and that has hampered this variety's commercial acceptance.

The apples can be kept refrigerated for up to four months after their harvest in September or October.

Jonamac

As the name advertises, this one is a cross between Jonathan and McIntosh. It was released in 1972 by the New York State Agricultural Experiment Station.

The skin is thin but persistent when chewed. The pale flesh is pleasantly firm and crisp, finely textured, and characterized by a tart but rounded taste that resembles Mac. A sweet, cidery aroma also calls Mac to mind.

Apples appear on the market late in September, shortly before McIntosh, and cannot be held for long in storage. Enjoy them as soon after harvest as possible.

Jonathan

Jonathan has come a long way since its discovery in Ulster County, New York, in the early 1800s. Within a hundred years it was the sixth best-selling apple in the United States, and it became Michigan's most popular variety. Jonathan's influence has been spread by a number of well-known crosses, most of them identifiable as family members because the names share the first four letters.

Jonathan can vary in flavor from mild to tart, depending on where it is grown. It has a spicy tang that some people also note in the apple's descendants. Beneath the thin, tough skin, the flesh is crisp, fine-textured, and juicy. It may be stained with red. This variety rates high for both eating fresh and cooking down into sauce, but it will not keep its shape when baked. Toss Jonathans into the hopper of a cider mill, and you'll retain something of their spicy character.

Jonathan ripens from mid-September through mid-October. The fruit does not keep particularly well.

Kandil Sinap

In a world of round or at least moderately orbicular apples, Kandil Sinap stands out. It may not stand up, however. That narrow base and cylindrical shape make it a comically tippy variety. (Even the tree is skinny.)

The apple is said to have originated in Turkey, where it dates back to the early 1800s. It's a gorgeous fruit. The brilliantly colored skin washes from red to yellow to green. It tastes good, too. The thin, tearing skin reveals white, finely textured flesh with an excellent balance between sweet and sour, scented with grapefruit.

Kandil Sinap is harvested in October and keeps quite well. It bruises easily.

Keepsake

Keepsake doesn't draw much attention to itself, but there is drama in its taste and aroma. Although the apple looks like an antique variety, it's a cross between Malinda and Northern Spy, introduced with northern growers in mind by the Minnesota Experiment Station in 1979.

The yellow-green flesh is fine-grained, hard, crisp, and breaking. The skin is somewhat chewy. Keepsake is full-flavored, with an invigorating sweet-tart balance. Both aroma and firmness moderate with storage after the October to November harvest and may be at their best early in the new year, by which time the flesh will have changed to a buttery yellow. In taste tests people have noted a melonlike aroma that pleases some and turns away others.

As the name promises, these apples keep very well. You'll have to stalk roadside stands for a sample, or buy a couple through the mail, because Keepsake is not as yet widely planted.

Kidd's Orange Red

This cross between Cox's Orange Pippin and Red Delicious bears the name of the man who bred it (as well as Gala and Freyberg), J. H. Kidd of New Zealand. The apple was introduced there in 1924. It picks up Cox's distinctive hue and has the heft of Delicious.

The flesh is warm white, crisp, juicy, and sweetly aromatic. To some tastes, Kidd's is superior to Gala, the better-known New Zealander, but russeting has limited its commercial appeal.

Kidd's ripens in late September and stores well through January.

King David

Stumbled upon a century ago as a chance fencerow seedling in Washington County, Arkansas, King David is thought to owe its deep hue to Arkansas Black, crossed with Jonathan. But the result looks and tastes enough like Winesap to suggest it, not Arkansas Black, as a parent.

King David has been called a sleeper. It was never grown in great numbers, but smaller orchards have shown new interest, and this variety may slip out from under its obscurity.

The cream-colored flesh is coarse, crisp, and possessed of a spicy, almost winelike flavor. The skin is rather tough. This is a good one for processing. Try it for golden yellow pies and sauce, and in cider.

The apples are ready for harvest in October and keep well.

King Luscious

An irregular hunk of an apple, with large, uneven lobes and a weight over a pound, King Luscious looks like a bland-tasting oaf but is a pleasant surprise. Although very few nurseries carry the tree, it is worth tracking down.

The variety is from a chance seedling, discovered in North Carolina in 1935. The apples ripen in October.

Knobbed Russet

This old-timer looks like a cross between Roxbury Russet and Idaho Russet—that is, between an apple and a potato. It was nearly a casualty of indifference. First spotted in Sussex, England, in 1819, the little oddball all but died out in the following century, to be saved by Britain's National Fruit Trials in the 1940s.

The dense pale gold flesh glistens with a pearly quality. Take a bite, and your tongue may recoil at first; that rough, toady skin feels as strange as it looks. The flavor is curiously pleasing, with an earthy taste and aroma that reinforce the initial impression of a subterranean heritage.

Knobbed Russet is harvested in October and keeps its quality well in storage. Growers tend to have troubles with it, making the variety all the harder to track down.

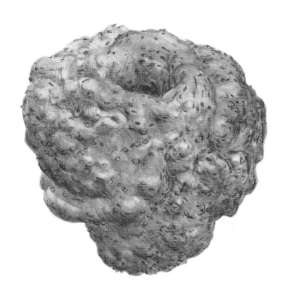

Lady

A small apple of many names, Lady is also known as Lady Apple, Lady Sweet, Christmas Apple, and Pomme d'Api. And its history is among the longest of any fruit variety, going back to the seventeenth-century orchards of Louis XIII and possibly beyond that to ancient Rome.

Lady's coloration varies greatly with exposure to sunlight. The flesh is paper white, crisp, and juicy. You might wonder if an apple this small could be satisfying. In fact, the intense flavor—a sunny sweetness like that of dried fruit, with a hint of citrus—makes up for there being few bites. This variety is unusual in that a good deal of its flavor and aroma is concentrated in the smooth skin.

Aside from its value as a dessert fruit, Lady has been a traditional choice at Christmas in centerpieces, garlands, and wreaths. In New England the apples were valued for cider.

Harvest may vary from late October through early December, and the fruit stays good for some months. They can survive freezing and thawing; that makes them all the better suited for wreaths on the front door.

Liberty

The name refers to the fruit breeders' goal of helping to liberate fruit growers from endless rounds of spraying. They've succeeded with Liberty. It has been called the most trouble-free of all apples. After years of tests it was introduced in 1978.

The New York State Agricultural Experiment Station crossed Macoun with an experimental variety to produce a deep red beauty with good flavor for eating out of hand. The pale yellow flesh is crisp, juicy, and flavorful and somewhat resembles Macoun. In a taste test at the University of Vermont Horticultural Research Center, Liberty scored first among five disease-resistant varieties and matched the scores of the much-praised Empire. Liberty holds on to its personality in recipes.

If you keep this apple cool after its October harvest, the flavor will increase over the next couple of months. Picked early, the fruit is apt to be disappointing.

McIntosh

McIntosh is the best-selling apple in the northeastern United States and in Canada. Unlike Red Delicious, the number one North American variety, it isn't the subject of snide remarks by apple aficionados.

John McIntosh, a farmer in Dundela, Dundas County, Ontario, Canada, gave his name to a talented cross between Fameuse and Detroit Red. The variety was introduced in 1870 and went on to much fame and much crossbreeding. McIntosh has lent its good genes to several well-known varieties, including Cortland, Empire, Macoun, and Spartan.

The original tree was badly scorched when a fire burned down the McIntosh farmhouse in 1894. But the old Mac limped on, yielding its last crop in 1908. It fell over two years later, and a stone memorial now marks the site.

The apple, in case you haven't visited your supermarket's produce section lately, has white, tender, crisp flesh that's spicy, highly aromatic, and full of juice. The characteristic flavor carries over into sauce, but in a pie the slices lose their shape. Macs are the principal cider apple in the Northeast.

Harvest is in September. Beware of McIntosh as winter wears on; the apples turn mealy if stored too long.

Macoun

Macoun has fans who hunt roadside stands each fall for a bushel or two. It is a prodigy of the New York State Agricultural Experiment Station, introduced in 1923 and named to honor a Canadian plant researcher (the name is pronounced ma-KOON). The apple has some resemblance, in taste and appearance, to its parent McIntosh (bred with Jersey Black) but with a darker red over the underlying green and a flavor that many prefer to Mac.

The white flesh is firm, aromatic, and juicy. This is a good pie apple.

Macoun is a variety that just doesn't sing if picked before or after the ideal harvest dates in late September or October. Buy from a market or grower you trust. The fruit bruises with rough handling.

Maiden Blush

This yellow variety develops crimson cheeks as the season comes to completion. Because Maiden Blush is attractive and can be highly aromatic uncut, the apples have been used atop fruit baskets.

Since its discovery in New Jersey some two centuries ago, Maiden Blush has been regarded as a multipurpose apple, suited to eating fresh, baking, making cider, and particularly drying (the slices stay light and attractive). The skin is resistant to the teeth, and the pale yellow flesh is crisp and tender. Massachusetts's Nashoba Valley Winery makes a Maiden Blush wine, tinting it with elderberries so that it looks like a so-called blush wine.

Crops ripen from mid-August through mid-September and store fairly well.

Melrose

You might expect the official apple of Ohio to have been around forever, but Melrose dates back only to World War II. It continues to be popular in that state, and some Ohio growers reserve their crops for regular customers. Melrose is not a flashy apple. The skin is a dull red and brightens with cooler temperatures in the northern part of its range.

This apple is a cross between Jonathan and Red Delicious, with firm, somewhat coarse, juicy flesh, warm white in color. It's sweet but offers a slight tartness and sturdy flavor that recommend it for recipes. Try Melrose in the kitchen; slices won't turn to mush in a pie and don't need much sweetener.

For fresh eating, hold off a couple of months after its October harvest date to allow the distinctively fruity aroma to reach its fullest. Melrose will keep quite well.

Mollie's Delicious

Mollie's was developed at Rutgers University, drawing on the genetic wealth of Golden Delicious and Red Gravenstein. It was introduced in 1966.

The greenish white flesh is crisp, sweet, and lively and apt to please those who favor a mild apple. Mollie's can be found widely at roadside markets in the Southeast, and to judge by the booming interest among mail-order nurseries, its reputation is spreading. Try the fruit in your favorite recipes.

The apples are harvested late in August and September and keep well for a summer variety. They are susceptible to bruising.

Mutsu

A Mutsu by any other name would taste just as sweet. But Western marketers have rechristened this Japanese variety Crispin to direct the shopper's attention toward the apple's excellent texture and away from its appearance.

Mutsu (pronounced moo-tsoo) is a cross of Golden Delicious and Indo, a Japanese seedling grown from a tree brought to Japan by an Indiana schoolteacher. It was developed in that country in the 1930s and arrived in the United States in the late 1940s.

The crisp white flesh is juicy and has a touch of tartness, for an excellent dessert apple. In taste tests of Golden Delicious and apples descended from it, Mutsu scores at the top. It does not make a particularly diverting pie. Sauce will have more flavor if you leave the peels on while cooking, then separate them with a strainer or colander. Mutsu is a worthwhile cider apple.

This apple should have a yellow background color. If the skin has a greenish cast, chances are the fruit was picked before their ideal October harvest date and won't have full flavor. Unlike Golden Delicious, the apples do not shrivel in storage.

Newtown Pippin

Newtown Pippin has been called the classic American apple. It holds the honor as the oldest commercially grown native variety in the United States. And it has a place in our lore, as the apple of George Washington's eye. Grafts found their way to Monticello, where Thomas Jefferson was eager to have the best and latest varieties.

The variety sprang from a seed in Newtown, Long Island. The original tree died when too many scions were cut from it for grafting. A greener version is known as Albemarle Pippin, named for the Virginia county, and Virginians claim it is more flavorful than Newtown.

Before Granny Smith invaded North America, Newtown was the best-appreciated green dessert apple. It continues to be enjoyed for a complexity that Granny lacks. Uncut, the apple may exhale a tangerine scent. The pale yellow flesh is crisp and tender, sweet on the tongue, and balanced by enough tartness. Some people detect a clean, pinelike quality. One minor drawback is that slices brown rapidly. Newtown makes a thick sauce, excellent pies with body, and a particularly clear cider.

Apples are ready to be picked in October, when they have warmed to a pale greenish yellow. They continue to get sweeter and richer in flavor for the next five months.

New York 429

This is one of hundreds of experimental varieties developed by state and provincial agricultural extensions, described only by number and known to a handful of people. Within these nameless ranks are many indifferent apples, many others notable only for a singular trait, and a few gems. The very best, in terms of both eating quality and marketing considerations, are given names and introduced to growers.

This apple, a cross between Red Spy and Empire, is one of the best. It was developed by the New York State Agricultural Experiment Station and soon will be named and made available.

The cream-colored flesh has inherited something of the spirit of Northern Spy, but the tartness of that variety has been muted; 429 carries the characteristic scent of McIntosh, a grandparent through Empire.

The harvest runs from September into October. The fruit remains flavorful and somewhat crisp into the New Year.

Northern Spy

Our consummate pie apple, say many people, and one of the best loved for eating out of hand as well. Yet Northern Spy is slipping from sight. As commercial growers concentrate on ever-fewer varieties, old favorites, especially stubborn ones like this apple, are forgotten.

The trees take up to a dozen years to get around to bearing and then are apt to produce a crop only every other year. The thin-skinned fruits are vulnerable to machines and better suited to time-intensive hand processing.

Spy had become the third most popular variety in the United States by the early 1900s. Since then the apple's range has shrunken. Most of its acreage is in New York, Michigan, and Ontario.

The yellowish white flesh is juicy and sweetly tart, with a high vitamin C content. Slices stay firm in a pie. This variety sprouted from a seed near Canandaigua, New York, around 1800. The site of the original tree, along a county road between Holcomb and Victor, is marked by a bronze plaque. Spy's parentage is unknown, but apple experts detect the influence of Wagener in its makeup.

The fruit is harvested in late September and into October. They'll keep their insides intact until spring, then surprise you with a taste of autumn. Be careful to avoid bruising them.

Northwestern Greening

The big yellow pie apple of the North, Northwestern is a cross between Golden Russet and Alexander that came out of Waupaca County, Wisconsin, in 1872. It is the most popular nonred apple grown in the North Central states.

Beneath Northwestern's tough skin, the greenish yellow flesh is firm, juicy, and mildly tart. This variety is best appreciated when cooked into sauce or pies and does not rate high eaten fresh.

The crop ripens in October. Northwestern has earned a reputation as a good keeper.

Ozark Gold

Ozark Gold is a beautiful, waxlike fruit, with a warm and even blush glowing over the bright lemon yellow skin. Burnished gold russeting crowns the top. The shape is unusual: a tall, flat-sided rectangle, as wide at the bottom as at the top.

Uncut, the apple may have a pearlike aroma. The fine-grained, snapping flesh is pale yellow in color and calls to mind Golden Delicious, the variety crossed with an unnamed apple by the Missouri State Agricultural Experiment Station to create Ozark. The fruit can be used for cooking as well as for eating fresh.

Apples are harvested from September through October and have an especially good flavor if tree-ripened. They store well.

Paradise

Also known as Paradise Sweet, this variety is believed to have come from Pennsylvania in the 1800s. Shards of the under-color show through a thin blush, for an unusual appearance.

The fine-grained flesh is juicy, lively on the tongue, and distinguished by a high concentration of sugar. Paradise has been valued as a drying apple.

The apples are picked in September and store well.

Pink Pearl

This novel apple is descended from Surprise, an old English variety named for the pink flesh that hides beneath its ordinary yellow exterior. Pink Pearl is also unremarkable at first glance, save for the warm glow imparted by the pink below the translucent skin.

The variety was developed in California by the well-known breeder Albert Etter and introduced in 1944. The color is more pronounced toward the northern part of its range. Pearl is crisp, tart, and aromatic, with a hint of grapefruit. It makes a pinkish sauce or pie filling.

In spring the blossoms are highly colored. The crop comes ripe in August or September and should be used fairly soon thereafter.

Pitmaston Pineapple

Although this variety has been overlooked for commercial use because of its modest size and russeted appearance, it once was known as a premier English dessert apple. Pitmaston dates to around 1780 and took its name from a town near Worcester, England.

The flesh is juicy and sweet and does, in fact, live up to its billing as pineapple-flavored, with the added suggestion of honey. Virginia grower Tom Burford says that if Pitmaston only were four times its size, it would be *the* russeted apple available today.

The crop is ready for harvest in mid-September and stores fairly well.

Prairie Spy

A multiuse apple that keeps through the winter, Prairie Spy was once widely sold but now is primarily a backyard orchardist's tree. Despite the name, it is not a relative of Northern Spy but has unknown parents and was brought into the world by the University of Minnesota Fruit Breeding Farm in 1940.

The crisp, medium-grained flesh is creamy white and may show some red veining. Prairie Spy rates as a good apple for eating fresh: juicy, flavorful, and lively on the tongue. You can use it in pies and sauce and store slices by freezing.

The apples ripen in October and keep their firmness and tartness until the end of the year. The aroma, however, tends to be more evanescent.

Red Delicious

You are looking at the most controversial apple grown in North America. Red Delicious has become a symbol (a distinctively shaped logo, you could say) of the American apple. It represents the industry that has made it a stereotype. It also says much about a people who drop more of them in their shopping carts than any other apple.

Red Delicious is a marketer's ideal: as intensely red as the apple in *The Sleeping Beauty*, instantly recognizable, tall and wasp-waisted, and gorgeous even after the insides have gone to mush. And big. Riding on those qualities, the variety has pushed regional favorites aside.

There is nothing imperialistic in this apple's genes, of course. It simply has been the lead player in our evolving notion of what an apple should be. The rise of Red Delicious has been called the victory of style over substance. Still, Big Red has its defenders, who point out that the original variety was a damned good apple. The skin is thick and bitter and has to be chewed vigorously. At its best the yellow flesh can be juicy, somewhat tart, and highly aromatic. This apple ranks close to the bottom when cooked.

Harvest is in September, but the apples are sold year-round, so shop with skepticism. Delicious retains its cheerful good looks long after the flavor has departed.

Rhode Island Greening

Green runs through and through this apple. It's said to have been started from seed in the 1600s by a Mr. Green, a tavern owner in Green's End, Rhode Island. The fruit itself has grass green skin, tending toward yellow and even orange with exposure to sun. Bite into one, and the tart, distinctively flavored flesh is revealed to be greenish white.

Rhode Island Greening ranks among the best American baking apples. A hundred years ago, when the home oven saw daily use, this variety was the second best seller in New York State. Greenings also are very good eaten out of hand, although they have been pigeonholed as a pie apple.

Harvest varies from September to late October. For baking and drying, the apples should be picked while firm. For eating fresh, however, a later harvest is best; the green will have yellowed, and the apple's tartness will be less aggressive. You can store Rhode Island Greenings for a few months.

Rome Beauty

Known also as simply Rome, this variety has a history that goes back to a fortuitous oversight. In the 1820s a tree planted along the northern bank of the Ohio River happened to send up a shoot from below the graft—from the part of the tree that is not supposed to bear fruit. Orchardists lop these unwanted shoots as routinely as they get haircuts. But this branch survived to bear splendidly colored fruit, and people began taking slips from it. The regionally famous tree was named for Rome Township, Ohio.

Sometime before the Civil War the waters rose up and washed the tree downriver. But by then Rome was well established. It continued to be grown more widely than many better-tasting varieties because of its size, conventionally handsome looks, and long shelf life.

Rome is a thick-skinned fruit that makes good eating but finds better use as a baker and in cider. The flesh, once you bite through to it, is crisp, firm, greenish white, and mildly tart.

Harvest is from late September into November. Beware of Romes that have become mealy and flavorless from storage.

Roxbury Russet

Roxbury Russet may be America's first pomological achievement, having been developed and named in Roxbury, Massachusetts, in the early 1600s.

A look at one suggests how the idea of a good apple has changed over the centuries. Roxbury presents a dull green, heavily marked face to the world. But the crisp, tart apple has more personality than some of today's supermarket standards. Its yellow-green flesh is firm and coarse-textured. Roxbury is suited to eating fresh and cooking and long has had a reputation as a fine cider apple.

Fruit is harvested from September into October. As with most russets, it keeps well for months, a characteristic that was highly valued in a day without refrigerators and commercial cold storage. Even after the skin feels soft to the touch, the insides may be satisfactorily crisp.

Senshu

This apple's unprepossessing appearance, along with a harvest date in the busiest part of the season, may hurt its commercial chances. Senshu is one of several recent introductions from Japan, a cross between Toko and Fuji that was brought out in 1980.

Whatever its fortunes in the marketplace, Senshu is an excellent dessert apple. Its crisp, juicy flesh tastes sweet and clean—something like Fuji but less firm. The skin may be a bit chewy.

Apples are harvested in September and have to be handled carefully to avoid bruising. They store fairly well but can't match Fuji's shelf life.

Spartan

Spartan is one of the McIntosh clan, being a cross between that parent and Newtown Pippin. It was developed by the British Columbia Experiment Station and introduced in 1936. The ribbed, dark, good-looking fruit buffs nicely. Uncut, it may have a sweet, candylike aroma.

The flesh is firm, crisp, snow white, and notably brisk in flavor and aroma. "I would like to see more people plant this one," says Tom Burford of Burford Brothers nursery, putting it near the top of the five hundred varieties he and his brother Russell offer. The flavor doesn't hold up well when cooked and has to lean on a lemon or two.

The apples are ready to pick in mid-October and should keep well for three months. Growers like Spartan for its disease resistance, and the variety is gaining in popularity.

Spigold

This large apple might also have been named Synergy for the way it borrows from and improves upon its genetic donors, Northern Spy and Golden Delicious. It was bred by the New York State Agricultural Experiment Station in Geneva and released in 1962.

Within a relatively short time Spigold has won a large following. It offers an excellent combination of Spy's crisp, sprightly flesh and the slightly herbal aromatic sweetness of its golden-hued parent. The result is a complex flavor that makes this apple stand out even in taste tests of a hundred varieties.

Spigold is the best-loved apple of many apple experts, including Roger D. Way, professor emeritus at the New York Experiment Station and the father of a few well-known varieties. Ed Fackler of Indiana's Rocky Meadow Orchard and Nursery, a man forever sampling old and new varieties, also names Spigold as his favorite.

The apples ripen from late September through November and stay good for up to three months.

Stayman

This seedling of Winesap was discovered by a Dr. J. Stayman of Leavenworth, Kansas, in 1866 and introduced by Stark Brothers nursery in 1895. With its underlying layer of green, Stayman shows a rich, muted red that suggests its parentage.

Stayman also shares Winesap's marked winy character, but in both flavor and texture it is a more accessible apple than Winesap. The greenish yellow flesh is firm, juicy, and aromatic. Try Stayman in recipes and cider.

The apples ripen in October and keep well. Note that apples sold as Winesap may in fact be Stayman.

Summer Rambo

The name sounds like an escapist movie sequel. But Summer Rambo is one of the oldest apple varieties, grown in the orchards of sixteenth-century Picardy, France, and brought to colonial America.

The flesh is yellowish green in color and particularly crisp and juicy, breaking off into slabs. The apples are often picked early and grass green for summer pies; at this stage they will be tart but may have so little aroma and taste when eaten fresh that you'd swear you had a head cold.

The fruit often shows vertical pale red stains on its sunny side if harvested mature, and a few in a basket may show a more pronounced blush. These fully ripe apples can offer a winy flavor that's satisfying eaten fresh. In parts of the United States, Rambo was known as the Bread and Cheese apple, a reference to its use as a dessert variety.

For pies, apples are picked in July. They become fully ripe from early August through early September and can be kept refrigerated for a few weeks.

SunCrisp

SunCrisp is a new apple without much of a history, but it has good breeding, including such ancestors as Cortland, Cox's Orange Pippin, and Golden Delicious.

Its skin is matte and dry to the touch, like that of Golden Delicious, and the uncut fruit shares this variety's scent as well. The skin is thin and unobtrusive. The golden flesh is crisp, firm, and fine-grained. SunCrisp tastes semitart and can be so full flavored and richly aromatic that "it screams a bit at you," in the words of Tom Vorbeck, who includes the apple among the dozens he sells by mail. At harvest the apple has a little too much character for some.

SunCrisp is harvested in October and keeps until January. Give it a month off the tree if you prefer a quieter apple.

Swaar

You have to be patient to enjoy this apple. It is best picked from the tree when still very firm, then allowed to soften and mellow before eating.

Swaar comes from New York's Hudson Valley, dating back at least two hundred years. The name means "heavy" in Dutch, a language that lingered on in that area from the days of rule by the Netherlands. And indeed, this is an unusually stolid apple. If it is stored until December, the firm white flesh becomes pleasing in texture and complex in flavor, with a good balance of sweet and tart.

The apples should be harvested in October and November, but you might leave some on the tree for the birds. Homeowners have set Swaar in the backyard expressly to feed wildlife.

Tompkins King

The birth statistics of many old apples have been obscured by time and the clutter of regional names. All that's known about this large, cheery apple is that the first seedling probably sprouted in Warren County, New Jersey, and was later introduced to Tompkins County, New York. By the early 1900s, when regional varieties still held sway, it was the number four apple in New York. Some orchards continue to grow it commercially.

The flesh is yellowish, crisp, juicy, and somewhat coarse. Tompkins is most often thought of as a cooking variety, but eaten out of hand, it appeals to those who like an aromatic, rich-tasting, sweet-tart apple. The fruit can develop a heavy, buttery quality, with an interesting aroma.

Tompkins is harvested in September or October. It rates as a good keeper and becomes greasy to the touch in storage.

Twenty Ounce

An apple weighing a pound and a quarter? Some Twenty Ouncers live up to the name. (Curiously, the variety is also known as Eighteen Ounce; the fruit illustrated here weighed in at two ounces shy of that.) Both New York State and Connecticut have been credited as the birthplace of this variety. It was introduced in the 1840s.

There are a couple of unusual tactile clues to the apple's identity. Its surface bears tiny indentations, or peening, as does Granny Smith. And the apples feel even heavier than they look.

The pale yellow flesh is fairly firm, tender, juicy, and somewhat tart. Twenty Ounce is not among the most intriguing of apples eaten fresh and is best enjoyed in recipes.

Apples ripen in September or October and should be used fairly soon after harvest.

Tydeman's Early

Tydeman's is one of the many varieties descended from McIntosh, crossed with Worcester Permain (after which it is also called Tydeman's Early Worcester). The breeding was done by Britain's East Malling Research Station, and Tydeman's had its launch in 1945. The variety found some success abroad, but it is not well known in America.

Beneath the thin, slick-feeling skin, the near-white flesh is firm and fine-textured, with a mild but engaging flavor and a novel perfumy sweetness that calls to mind cotton candy. Tydeman's might not become your favorite everyday apple, but it makes an interesting diversion. A grafted limb should satisfy a backyard grower's appetite for the apple. Tydeman's rates as a good cooking variety.

The crop starts ripening late in August and continues for some weeks.

Wagener

With its lobes and coloration, Wagener can look like a not-quite-ripe tomato. It was discovered in 1791 as a seedling near Penn Yan, in the fruitful Finger Lake district of New York State. Wagener perpetuates the name of the man who propagated the variety.

The shape is unusual, being decidedly asymmetrical and having five sides. The skin is greasy to the touch and marked by slight peening, and it may show long, thin, sinuous lines of russeting scattered here and there.

Uncut, the apple has a slight cidery aroma. The flesh is crisp, tender, fine-grained, and juicy. Wagener has some tartness and is quite aromatic, with a flavor that calls Northern Spy to mind. (A family resemblance suggests that Spy is an offspring.) This is a good variety to cook down into applesauce, and it comes recommended highly as a cider apple.

The apples ripen in October and keep well.

Wealthy

Wealthy is thought to be a cross between Cherry Crab and Sops of Wine and was discovered in the mid-1800s near Excelsior, Minnesota. Commercial production has slipped since the early 1900s, but this apple continues to be popular in the North Central states.

The greenish white flesh may be stained pink under the skin and is rather soft and coarse in texture. Wealthy has a lively flavor and sweet fragrance. It is an all-purpose workhorse, suited for eating fresh, making pies and sauce, pressing for cider, and freezing and baking.

The apples are harvested in September and won't stay interesting if stored for long.

Westfield Seek-No-Further

This one arouses passion with its taste, not with its looks. Russeting can blanket the apple so that the skin just peeks through, and there is a bluish bloom overall.

Westfield was identified as something special in eighteenth-century Massachusetts (it's named for a town in that state). Although once a popular New England apple, it is now seldom grown.

The flavor is astringent and memorable, buffered by an aroma unique to the variety. The pale yellow-green flesh is crisp and juicy and browns rapidly. The skin is rather tough. Virginia grower Tom Burford has noted that in tastings, people either become glassy-eyed with enchantment over Westfield or declare it a "spitter" and move on to the next sample. Although best known as a dessert apple, Westfield can be used in recipes.

Apples are picked from September through November. They store a short while before losing their stuff.

White Winter Pearmain

White Winter Pearmain is a venerable English variety that has been traced back to A.D. 1200, which would make it the oldest-known English apple.

This variety's waxy, somewhat tough skin yields to a crisp, tender, fine-grained flesh. Its flavor is rich and aromatic, earning the sobriquet "poor man's Mutsu" for a similarity to that modern Japanese apple. Apple lore has it that White Winter was one of the most popular dessert varieties on midwestern farms. It makes good cider.

Harvest is from late September through October. The apples stay good for months.

Winesap

Winesap is the distillation of a crisp fall day. The apple has character—too much character for some. Beneath its sturdy skin, the yellow flesh is firm, toothsome, and very juicy, with a powerful sweet-sour contrast and the characteristic winy flavor and aroma. Winesap serves well in the kitchen, and its flavor carries over into sauce, pie, and cider. Note that its famously invigorating personality may be missing in areas where local climate or soil conditions are not favorable.

Winesap is thought to have come from New Jersey. By 1817 it was recorded as an important cider apple in that state. Its popularity spread, and Winesap remained a major late-season apple until the mid-1900s, when controlled atmosphere storage made it possible to offer many varieties in its season. But Winesap continues to be widely grown, in spite of its relatively small size and competition from a milder offspring, Stayman.

Apples are ready for harvest between late September and early November and remain enjoyable for months. In blossom a row of Winesaps will glow pinker than most.

Winter Banana

Is the beautiful lemon yellow, waxy skin responsible for the name? Or does this apple really taste like a banana, as some commentators insist?

Even sensitive and experienced noses may miss any hint of banana in Winter Banana's rich aroma, which is as you might expect of a seedling found growing on a farm in Cass County, Indiana. But its good looks are undeniable, and Winter Banana has been featured in fruit baskets.

The skin is highlighted with anything from a pale alizarin blush to an intense rouge that looks as though it had been spray-painted. The apple is often peppered with flecks of near black and bright carmine. A further distinguishing mark may be a suture line.

The uncut fruit has a faint, flowery perfume. Inside, the firm flesh is mild, crisp, and juicy. Winter Banana becomes rather unexciting when cooked but it makes a good cider apple.

The crop ripens from late September through October. The apples turn greasy and mealy with storage and can't be held on to for very long. Handle them gingerly to avoid bruising the skin.

Wolf River

In 1875 a seedling along the banks of the lower Wolf River near Fremont, Wisconsin, caught the eye of a person who knew apples. The tree is thought to have sprung from a Russian apple, Alexander. The variety remains popular in the upper Midwest.

Wolf River is best known as a kitchen talent, particularly for apple butter, and may be dried to good advantage. Still, growers say that this big apple can yield a good out-of-hand experience if the trees receive full sun and are grown in sandy soil. The warm white flesh is soft and tends to become mealy, but the slightly tart flavor has character.

Harvest dates vary from August into October. The apples can't be stored very long, and fruits left on the tree rapidly degenerate. Unlike most varieties, Wolf River grows relatively true from seed.

Yellow Bellflower

Shake this good-size lemon yellow fruit, and you may be surprised by the hollow rattle of seeds within. Yellow Bellflower has been traced to a field along Crosswicks Creek in northern Burlington County, New Jersey, sometime in the 1700s. The warm white flesh is crisp, firm, and somewhat finely grained; right off the tree, the apple has a sweet flavor that's offset by a hint of tartness, and you might note some starchiness as well. In the kitchen Yellow Bellflower can be used for pies and sauce, and it is a good cider ingredient.

The fruit is picked in September or October and will bruise if juggled. Allow them some time in cold storage to resolve the starchy character. Should you be considering apple trees for the lawn, this one's blossoms are large and especially attractive.

York Imperial

York apples look as though they were leaning into a strong wind. That lopsided shape can be mistaken for a flaw—and unknowing agricultural inspectors have rejected truckloads for this reason alone—but it is characteristic of the variety. In the Pennsylvania German dialect used around the apple's York County birthplace, it was called a schepabbel, or crooked apple.

York dates to around 1830. The gaudy "Imperial" was added to its name for a homely virtue: long storage life. The apple has faint vinous smell before being cut. It will disappoint you if "tart" and "tangy" are adjectives you associate with a proper apple. The coarse-grained yellowish flesh is firm, crisp, and juicy—pleasant in its own right.

York excels in the kitchen and as a cider apple. It was once the best-selling variety in the Appalachians from Pennsylvania south through Virginia and remains a popular processing apple in that region, in part because of an unusually small core. The warm-hued flesh lends a rich look to pies and sauce.

The fruit is ready to be picked in October. Fans of York say the apple improves in character through to the end of the year, but you may find that it merely holds its own.

Zabergau Reinette

Brown like a nut, and tastes like a nut (a little). Zabergau came from Württemberg, Germany, in the 1880s. The fine-grained white flesh is crisp, full-flavored, and not to everyone's taste.

Nor is the fruit's appearance, with its heavy russeting doing a fair impersonation of a moonscape. The term *reinette* suggests as much; it is thought to be from the French *raine*, a tree frog noted for its spotted skin.

The apples begin to become ripe in September and can be harvested over a period of weeks. They hold up well in storage.

❖   ❖   ❖

Antique apple. An old variety that has become obscure or non-commercial. Most were discovered as trees growing from seeds, rather than having been developed intentionally.

Baggers. Apples that are smaller than the standard size for their variety and are marketed relatively inexpensively in plastic bags.

Bloom. The dusty blue, gray, or white coating of wax on an apple. The bloom on most apples destined for the supermarket has been buffed to a shine; you can do the same on a shirt sleeve.

Dessert apple. A variety particularly suited to eating out of hand—that is to say, uncooked.

Grafting. Attaching a SCION of one plant to another plant.

Greasy. Used to describe the slick-to-the-touch waxy coat that develops on certain varieties in storage. It generally can be taken as a sign that the apple is nearing the end of its prime, but some varieties will still be crisp and flavorful inside.

Greening. A traditional term for apples that are green when mature.

Heavy in hand. Have you noticed that some varieties seem heavier, for their size, than others? In fact, orchardists do speak of "hand heavy" apples that have a higher specific gravity. A couple of summer varieties, Lodi and Yellow Transparent, are conspicuously light. Blue Permain, Spigold, and Swaar are relative heavyweights.

Introduce. To offer a named apple variety to the commercial trade.

Mealy. Used to describe apple flesh that has broken down and lost its crispness.

Pearmain. A loosely described class of apple varieties, with several possible derivations: apples with a long and vaguely pearlike shape; those with firm, pearlike flesh; those with a characteristic flavor; and those coming from Parma, Italy.

Peening. Tiny indentations on the surface of an apple, characteristic of certain varieties.

Pippin. See SEEDLING.

Reinette. An apple characterized by a spotted appearance.

Rootstock. The root system on which GRAFTING is done.

Russet. An apple characterized by extensive russeting, a rough, corky material that forms over the skin.

Scion. A small part of a tree that is removed and attached by GRAFTING to another tree. This part will grow to bear fruit of the donor's variety. One tree may be grafted to several apple varieties.

Seedling. A variety, or an individual tree, that grew from a seed rather than having been reproduced by GRAFTING to a ROOTSTOCK.

Sport. A genetic aberration on part of a tree.

Strain. A variation within a variety. Royal Gala is a strain of the variety Gala.

Subacid. A slightly tart flavor.

Suture. A line running over the skin from top to bottom. It is characteristic of some varieties, and occasionally caused on others by growing conditions.

Sweet-tart (or tart-sweet). A flavor that combines sweet and sour.

Typy. Conforming closely to the appearance of a well-known commercial apple.

Variety. A variation on a species. For example, Golden Delicious is a variety of *Malus domestica*. Varieties are named or, in experimental programs, identified by number.

SOURCES

❖   ❖   ❖

MAIL-ORDER APPLES

Applesource
Tom Vorbeck
Route 1
Chapin, IL 62628
An easy way to educate your palate and to test a variety before planting it.

MAIL-ORDER TREES

For a complete list of varieties for sale, see the latest edition of *Fruit, Berry and Nut Inventory*, issued by Seed Saver Publications, 3076 North Winn Road, Decorah, IO 52101.

Alliance Nursery
5965 Alliance Road
Marianna, FL 32448
Varieties for southern climates.

Bear Creek Nursery
PO Box 411
Northport, WA 99157

Burford Brothers
Monroe, VA 24574
Some five hundred varieties.

C and O Nursery
PO Box 116
Wenatchee, WA 98807–0116

Chestnut Hill Nursery
Route 1, Box 341
Alachua, FL 32615
Varieties for southern climates.

Cloud Mountain Farm
6906 Goodwin Road
Everson, WA 98247

Fruit Testing Association Nursery, Inc.
PO Box 462
Geneva, NY 14456
The backyard grower's access to experimental trees from the
New York State Experiment Station.

Just Fruits Nursery
Route 2, Box 4818
Crawfordville, FL 32327
Varieties for southern climates.

Lawson's Nursery
Route 1, Box 472
Yellow Creek Road
Ball Ground, GA 30107
Northern Georgia varieties.

Henry Leuthardt Nurseries
Montauk Highway, Box 666
East Moriches, NY 11940
This Long Island company also sells espalier trees and fences at the nursery.

Long Hungry Creek Nursery
Jeff Poppen
Red Boiling Springs, TN 37150
Specializes in disease-resistant varieties.

Miller Nurseries
West Lake Road
Canandaigua, NY 14424

Northwoods Nursery
28696 South Cramer Road
Molalla, OR 97038

Raintree Nursery
391 Butts Road
Morton, WA 98356

Rocky Meadow Orchard and Nursery
360 Rocky Meadow Road NW
New Salisbury, IN 47161

St. Lawrence Nurseries
RD 2
Potsdam, NY 13676
Varieties for northern climates.

Sonoma Antique Apple Nursery
4395 Westside Road
Healdsburg, CA 95448

Southmeadow Fruit Gardens
Lakeside, MI 49116
Sells a chatty, informative catalog.

Stark Bros. Nursery
Highway 54, PO Box 10
Louisiana, MO 63353

Swedberg Nurseries
Box 418
Battle Lake, MN 56515
Varieties for northern climates.

CIDER PRESSES

Burford Brothers
Monroe, VA 24574

Correll Cider Presses
24791 Warthen Road
Elmira, OR 97437

WINEMAKING SUPPLIES

New York Homebrew
36 Cherry Lane
Floral Park, NY 11001

Tri-Bio Labs
1400 Fox Hill Road
State College, PA 16801

The Wine Lab
1200 Oak Avenue
St. Helena, CA 94574

BOOKS

The Apple Book, by Rosanne Sanders (Philomel Press, 1988). A beautifully illustrated British book of apple varieties, showing foliage and blossoms as well as the fruit, with technical descriptions.

Apples: A Catalog of International Varieties
Burford Brothers
Monroe, VA 24574
Descriptions of many varieties by a family that has grown apples for several generations.

Apples of New York, by S. A. Beach (1905)
An illustrated, two-volume descriptive listing of more than one thousand varieties. Long out of print, but available through used-book sellers.

Fruit, Berry and Nut Inventory
Seed Saver Publications
3076 North Winn Road
Decorah, IO 52101
A descriptive list, in paperback form of more than one thousand apple varieties sold by mail-order nurseries in the United States and Canada.

Sweet and Hard Cider, by Annie Proulx and Lou Nichols (Garden Way Press, 1980).

American Pomological Society
103 Tyson Building
University Park, PA 16802
Publishes *Fruit Varieties Journal.*

The North American Fruit Explorers
Jill Vorbeck
Route 1, Box 94
Chapin, IL 62628
Publishes a quarterly journal, *Pomona*, and runs a mail-order library of fruit books and articles. Open to amateurs and professionals.

Pomona Book Exchange
H. Fred Janson
Highway 552
Rockton P. O.
Ontario LOR 1XO
Canada

Rodale Institute Research Center
611 Siegfriedale Road
Kutztown, PA 19530
Studies organic apple pest management.

ACKNOWLEDGMENTS

❖   ❖   ❖

Thanks to Tom Burford of Burford Brothers, Monroe, Virginia, for going over the paintings and spotting the Ralls Janet pretender; to Roger D. Way, Pomology Emeritus, New York State Agricultural Experiment Station, Cornell University, Geneva, New York, for reviewing the text; to Tom and Jill Vorbeck of Applesource, for their comments on the text, and box after box of apples almost too pretty to eat; to Don Ziegler, for gathering a fascinating grab bag of varieties on his annual orchard tour of the Midwest; to Allen and Marguerite Hobert of Hoberts Orchards, Landis Store, Pennsylvania, for their advice; to Amos Fisher, Bob Seip, David Belles, and Eric Habbeger of Back Yard Fruit Growers; to Ed Fackler of Rocky Meadow Orchard and Nursery; to Theo C. J. Grootendorst of Southmeadow Fruit Gardens; to H. Fred Janson; to John Hillbrand, librarian of the North American Fruit Explorers; to Phil Forsline of the Plant Genetic Research Unit, Geneva, New York; and to my children, Metthea and Rhodes, who sampled some 150 varieties and never complained of an upset stomach.